THROUGH THE YEAR WITH OSCAR ROMERO

THROUGH THE YEAR
WITH OSCAR ROMERO

Daily Meditations

Translated by Irene B. Hodgson, Ph.D.

Franciscan
MEDIA
Cincinnati, Ohio

This book originally appeared in Spanish as *Día a día con Monseñor Romero: Meditaciones para todo el año*, copyright © 1999, 2000, by Publicaciones Pastorales del Arzobispade, Colonia Escalón, San Salvador

Cover and book design by Mark Sullivan
Cover photo © Leif Skoogfors/CORBIS

LIBRARY OF CONGRESS CATALOGING-IN-PUBLICATION DATA
(from 2005 edition)
Romero, Oscar A. (Oscar Arnulfo), 1917-1980.
[Día a día con Monseñor Romero. English]
Through the year with Oscar Romero : daily meditations / translated by Irene B. Hodgson.
p. cm.
ISBN 0-86716-695-9 (alk. paper)
1. Devotional calendars—Catholic Church. 2. Catholic Church—Prayer-books and devotions—English. I. Title.
BX2170.C56R6613 2005 242'.2—dc22
2005000287

ISBN 978-1-63253-065-3

English translation copyright © 2005, by Franciscan Media.
This edition published November 2015.
All rights reserved.
Translated from the Spanish by Irene B. Hodgson, Ph.D.

Published by Franciscan Media
28 W. Liberty Street
Cincinnati, OH 45202
www.AmericanCatholic.org

Printed in the U.S.A.
15 16 17 18 19 5 4 3 2 1

Prologue to the Spanish Edition

Twenty years later and on the verge of a new millennium, Archbishop Romero's words continue to be current. His homilies continue to challenge us and make demands on us, they continue giving us spirit and hope. No one who reads or listens to his homilies today can remain indifferent. And it is because Archbishop Romero's words, like those of the Gospel, continue to be current because they are prophetic words, the "echo" of God in the people of El Salvador.

On this occasion we present a selection of texts from his homilies. There are 365 texts, one for each day of the year. The intention is for this book to become a book for daily meditation, so that Archbishop Romero might accompany us throughout the year. He himself, on one occasion, suggested to us that we move to that "intimate space" of our conscience to encounter ourselves there, then to go out and encounter our poor people. If Archbishop Romero was able to say such clear words, to love the poor and offer his own life, it was because always, however busy he was, he spent time in meditation and personal prayer.

The texts selected have been chosen from the first edition of the homilies of Archbishop Romero that was previously published by the Archdiocese of San Salvador: *Archbishop Oscar Romero: His Thought* (8 volumes). At the end of each text, we indicate the date from which the selection was taken. For those people who want to study Archbishop Romero's thought more deeply, we recommend reading his homilies and pastoral letters.

"Brothers and sisters, keep this treasure. It is not my poor word that sows hope and faith; I am no more than the humble echo of God in this people" (October 2, 1977). Let us honor, then, this treasure, the great legacy that he left us. Let us bring his words to life in our own lives, let us be human and Christian like Monseñor Romero was and let us build a country like the one of which he dreamed.

Introduction to the English edition

Bishop Ricardo Urioste
Holy Week of 1980 was a true Passion Week in El Salvador. In the city center—the cathedral—a bloody Golgotha was enacted. A body to bury in a new tomb was the circumstance that unleashed the tragedy. Days before, Monday, March 24, it had all begun in the chapel of a small hospital with the horrendous assassination of Archbishop Romero while he was celebrating the Eucharist.

The most inhuman "laws" are those that are never announced publicly—like the one that ordered the assassination of Archbishop Romero. Like the one that ordered the evil of the century at the cathedral.[*] Like the one that ordered—because someone must have ordered it—the assassination of more than 70,000 Salvadorans.

---

* The crowd at Romero's funeral overflowed the cathedral and filled the plaza outside. Thirty people were killed and four hundred wounded when the army opened fire on the crowd.

During his trip to the United States in October of 1979, Pope John Paul II said:

> The social thought and the social practice inspired by the Gospel will always be characterized by a sensitivity toward those who suffer most, those who are extremely poor, those who are overwhelmed by all the physical, mental and moral evils that afflict humanity, including hunger, contempt, unemployment and despair. You need to look for the structural causes that promote the different classes of poverty in the world.

Archbishop Romero was killed because of what he preached and what he said. But he never said anything that was not consistent with the Gospel and with the teachings of the Church. If these have been given to us, it is clearly so that they be carried out. At least, that is the way Archbishop Romero understood it. He was not one who accepted things "calmly" or "with prudence." He was faithful to the Gospel and Church teachings. He died for them. "To feel with the church" was not merely a pretty phrase for him. His guide was the Second Vatican Council, Medellín, Puebla and all the Church teachings.[**]

No one can find in his innumerable sermons a single phrase that is not supported by the Gospel and Church teaching, applied to the situation in which his people lived. He never said anything of which he was not firmly convinced.

Because of this, "he was clearly guilty." The world has never tolerated men like this. The world tolerates and accepts those

---

[**] "To feel with the Church" was Romero's motto as Archbishop. Medellín and Puebla were the sites for the Latin American Bishops' Conference meetings in 1968 and 1979.

who are mediocre, those who are complacent. Those like Monseñor are hung on a cross, alongside thieves. They are considered criminals and disturbers of the peace.

The one who spoke out the most about defending life in El Salvador did not want to defend his own life. He only wanted to be faithful as a Good Shepherd.

Monseñor was known for taking things seriously. This is the way that the Church wants us to take them, since it asks this of us in its documents. He had brought the motto of his life— "to feel with the Church"—to what was happening and he had let himself be enveloped by the universal teaching of the Church. He loved the pope with all his heart—no matter which pope—and made the teachings of the church his own.

This book speaks of what Archbishop Romero said and preached. This book speaks of him, of the church and of the suffering people. He wanted to make his own what the pope and the Latin American Bishops in Puebla said: "Not all of us in Latin America have committed ourselves enough to the poor, we are not always concerned about them and in solidarity with them.... We affirm the need for conversion of the whole Church for a preferential option for the poor, with a view to their integral liberation" (Puebla, 1134).

That you are with the poor and love them must be proved by your actions. Archbishop Romero gave very clear examples of this and that is why he was killed. A better way to say it would be that he gave his life for this. He was a martyr of his faithfulness to the Church teaching, to the poor, to Christ and to the Church. From this came his actions; his sorrows were the lack of understanding of those who never understood what it means to truly be converted.

This book contains excerpts from the homilies of Archbishop Romero, from his three years as Archbishop of San Salvador. They are designed to be read, prayed about, and meditated on. More than anything, they are a plea, a desire, a cry toward earth and toward God. Transcendence, prayer, the dignity of men and women, conversion, the rich, and the poor are topics he discusses. He loved the Church, he loved Christ, and he deeply loved his people.

Because of this, on the day after Monseñor's death, the pope said:

> In this way he crowned with blood his ministry that was especially concerned with the poorest and most marginalized. It was a supreme witness that has provided a symbol of the torment of the people, but also a cause to hope for a better future.

Translator's Introduction

A translation of *Día a día con Monseñor Romero* (literally *Day by Day with Archbishop Romero*) was first requested for the twenty-fifth anniversary of the death of Archbishop Oscar Romero, "Monseñor," "San Romero de América," in 2005 by Bishop Ricardo Urioste, head of the Romero Foundation. At that time, El Salvador was still ruled by the ARENA party whose founder had been named by the United Nations Truth Commission Report as the person in El Salvador who had arranged for Romero's murder—although the report also suggested that the order had come to him from Miami. In 2009, the FMLN, Frente Farabundo Martí para la Liberación Nacional, which had been the umbrella organization for five guerrilla groups trying to overthrow the government of El Salvador transformed into a political party after a negotiated settlement to the civil war and the signing of Peace Accords, won its first presidential election with Mauricio Funés, a candidate who had not previously been a *guerrilla*, nor even a member of the FMLN party. Elected in 2014, the current president is Salvador Sánchez Cerén, who *had* been a *guerrilla* commander. The failed

U.S. policy had provided massive aid to shore up one repressive government after another in a country with great social and economic inequalities with a large group of landless peasants and a small elite. This led to civil war in 1980, the year Romero, Salvadoran political and labor leaders and four U.S. churchwomen were killed either by official government forces or the death squads created by the founder of the ARENA party. The war led to major migration of Salvadorans to the U.S. and other places as the twelve-year civil war dragged on. Of the one million who came to the U.S., the vast majority were in the Los Angeles area. As young Salvadorans were deported after the war, the L.A. gang-culture accompanied them to El Salvador. Gang violence has increased recently in El Salvador.

When Oscar Romero was named Archbishop of San Salvador in 1977 after the retirement of Luis Chávez y González, he seemed to be the safe choice, someone who would not rock the boat in the way that his predecessor had, and, as it was feared, other possible candidates might. While some, especially Passionist priests Zacarías Diez and Juan Macho in their book *En Santiago de María me tope con la miseria: dos años de la vida de monseñor Romero (1975-1976): años de cambio?,* argue that he already was well on the road to becoming a voice for justice based on his experience as bishop of Santiago de María (1974-1977), it is clear that his commitment and voice grew after the death of Father Rutilio Grande, S.J.—also mentioned as a martyr for the faith by Pope Francis. Grande was ambushed and killed along with an old man and a little boy on March 12, 1977. Romero's decision to cancel all but one Mass in the archdiocese on the Sunday after the deaths was significant. Jon Sobrino, S.J., Spanish Basque theologian at the Jesuit Central American University who has spent most of his life in El Salvador, has written:

Whether one actually calls it a conversion or not, the radical change that took place in Archbishop Romero on the occasion of Rutilio's murder was one of the most impressive things anyone around him, including myself has ever seen...I believe that the murder of Rutilio Grande was the occasion of the conversion of Archbishop Romero—as well as being a source of light and courage.

In his homilies, Romero discussed in detail the texts for the day, but he also denounced situations of injustice. El Salvador was a country in which traditionally 2 percent of the population (the so-called "fourteen families") controlled over 90 percent of the wealth. The largest group (up to 60 percent) were landless peasants. Romero pleaded with the wealthy to change the system or face civil war. He spoke out more and more strongly, becoming known as "the voice of the voiceless." Shortly before his death, he asked U.S. president Jimmy Carter to stop sending aid to the Salvadoran government that, he emphasized, was used only to repress and kill its people. On March 23, 1980, in his last Sunday homily, he appealed to members of the Salvadoran military to not obey orders contrary to the laws of God and to stop killing their brothers and sisters. It is popularly believed that this led directly to his death the next day, but his death was already planned; lots had been drawn as to who was to kill him. It had been announced in the newspaper that on March 24 Archbishop Romero would be the celebrant for Mass for the one-year anniversary of the death of the mother of beleaguered newspaper editor Jorge Pinto at the Divine Providence chapel of the cancer hospital for indigents where Romero had a small house. Romero was struck in the heart by an assassin's exploding bullet and died before reaching a hospital.

That same year, four U.S. churchwomen and numerous political leaders and leaders of popular organizations were also killed. The more progressive forces saw no alternative but to go underground and join the FMLN—the Farabundo Martí Front for National Liberation was the umbrella organization for five guerrilla groups and was named for the leader of an abortive uprising in 1932 when thousands were murdered in what is called "La Masacre," the Massacre. Unlike the U.S.-backed *contras* in Nicaragua trying to overthrow the Sandinista government, the *guerrillas* ended up controlling large areas of the country and finally brought the war to the capital city of San Salvador in 1989. The government troops bombed poor area of the city so that their inhabitants would not give aid and shelter to the guerrilla forces. The special forces Atlacatl Battalion entered the Central American University and killed six Jesuit priests, who were calling for a negotiated settlement, along with a staff member and her daughter, who were witnesses.

Eventually, there was a negotiated end to the war, peace accords, a United Nations' Truth Commission and the first presidential elections after the war in 1994. However, the economic inequalities and many of the social problems that caused the war, continued.

The process of Romero's beatification stagnated as questions were raised about whether he was a martyr for the faith or had been killed for political reasons until it was recently accelerated by Pope Francis, the first Latin American pope, when Pope Francis declared him to be a martyr for the faith. Although the process was slow, as Jon Sobrino, S.J., wrote in an article for the tenth anniversary of Romero's death, Romero had already been sainted by the people who called him "San Romero de América," St. Romero of America and began to write songs and poems about him. According to Sobrino, the places Romero lived and died—on the grounds of the cancer hospital for indigents, his little house and the Divine Providence chapel where he was killed, his tomb in the cathedral (in each of the three locations)—as well as the date of his death—are considered holy. His death has come to represent that of all the martyrs—including those killed when government troops opened fire on the crowd at his funeral. When the people of El Salvador say "Monseñor" with no last name attached, they are referring to Romero. ("Monseñor Romero" is often mistranslated in English as "Monsignor Romero." In Spanish, the direct address title used for bishops and above is "monseñor"; Romero was a bishop and then the archbishop of San Salvador; he never held the rank of monsignor.) In his testimony in *Vida y muerte en Morazán*, Belgian priest Rogelio Ponceele describes conflicts between Romero and more progressive communities and priests in an earlier period and how that changed "when Monseñor had become Monseñor." Father Ignacio Ellacuría, like Jon Sobrino a Spanish Basque, rector of the UCA when he was murdered on November 16, 1989, said at a mass to honor Romero that "with Romero, God passed through El Salvador."

During Romero's tenure as archbishop, his Sunday homilies were broadcast on the archdiocesan radio station which was the target of attacks that seemed designed to keep his words from reaching the people. Romero spoke from notes, but his homilies were later transcribed and published. María Julia Hernández, head of the archdiocesan human rights office Tutela Legal, told me in 1990 when I was translating Romero's diary that the transcription began when she suggested that Archbishop Romero use the text of one of his homilies as his Christmas greeting one year.

James Brockman, S.J., author of *Romero: A Life* (previously *Oscar Romero: The Word Remains*) and *the Violence of Love*, was reading the homilies and publishing excerpts of Romero's prophetic voice in English. For the twentieth anniversary of Romero's death in 2000, the archdiocese published a multivolume set including the homilies, Romero's diary and a small book, *Día a día con monseñor Romero*, a compilation of excerpts from the homilies designed for daily meditation. As a set, it was too expensive for many Salvadorans struggling to survive.

I first saw *Día a día* for sale by itself at the twenty-fourth anniversary celebration in March of 2004. It only cost three or four dollars, but this was a great deal of money for many Salvadorans when entire families in extreme poverty live on one to two dollars a day. When I went to mass in the crypt of the cathedral, near the second location for Romero's tomb, in late September 2004, all of the readings that were not from Scripture were from this book, and I heard a man asking how much it cost. Then he said that he did not have enough that day but that he hoped to have enough money to buy it within a few weeks. When I gave some copies in March 2004 to people in communities in Nicaragua, they clutched them to their breasts and said reverently that they had never had Romero's actual words in their hands before. This little book made Romero's words available to the people in a way it had never had been before—like liberation theology made the Biblical texts accessible to people.

When Guillermo Cuéllar, author and composer of the Salvadoran Folk Mass (1980) and the Mesoamerican Mass (2000), approached me on behalf of Bishop Urioste and the Romero Foundation about translating *Día a día* into English, he told me that it should be a poetic translation, freer, less literal, more like the oral interpretation I had done for him at concerts and reflections as well as a written translation of his Mesoamerican Mass that continues to evolve. The hope was for it to be accessible to an English-speaking audience to be used for meditation--but without changing Archbishop Romero's thoughts. As mentioned earlier, Romero usually spoke from notes rather than from a prepared text. Most of the texts we have, both of his homilies and his diary, are transcriptions of recordings rather than finished written texts. He uses a good many sentence fragments and juxtaposes and paraphrases ideas from the Bible. Like with my earlier translation of his diary which had originally been recorded on cassette tapes, I imagined myself interpreting orally as I work. The last step in my process of working on a translation of a work that was originally oral is to read the translations aloud, and, if different words fit better in my mouth that the ones I had written down, I change the text accordingly. This may mean that occasionally the level of language may change a little, become more popular, a little less formal so as to not sound stilted in English. I may translate "those" as "these"; Spanish idiomatic expressions may be transformed into equivalent English idiomatic expressions, and the order of words in a sentence may change.

When I first began translating texts by Latin American theologians at the request of Dr. Paul Knitter of the Xavier University department of theology, he asked me to make the language inclusive. In Spanish, traditionally, if a term is mean to include both masculine and feminine, the endings (and the pronouns) are masculine. If this were not changed in English, the English translation would be less inclusive than the Spanish. When Archbishop Romero says *hermanos*, I have translated it as "brothers and sisters," except when he is clearly referring to his "brother priests." I have rendered *hombres* as "human beings" or "human-kind." Often when he uses "one" or "he," I have translated this in the plural so that the text is not overly peppered with phrases like "she or he" of "his or her," "him or her." I have used both "shepherd" and "pastor" in English for the Spanish "pastor" which actually means both, depending on how he seemed to be using it at the moment. I have usually translated "monseñor" as "bishop" or "archbishop" since, as indicated above, "monseñor" in Spanish is the title of address for bishops, archbishops, monsignors and cardinals and its use does not mean that the person in question holds the rank of monsignor. I have left "Monseñor" in a few places, especially in Bishop Urioste's introduction when it is used as Romero's name and when the use of "bishop" or "archbishop" would create too much of a distance not there in the Spanish.

Many of these changes occur naturally in oral translation to keep the vitality and passion of living words. Romero speaks often in these texts of the Gospel for "today" and of how a text is not a museum piece. Some who know Spanish and read this book in both Spanish and English may say, "Oh, I wouldn't have said it that way," or "He is a product of his time. Leave the language alone." There is often more than one way of saying the same thing, but, as I have said above, preserving the Spanish gender conventions in English would make the language *less* inclusive than the original.

From my work translating his diary over twenty years ago, I know that Archbishop Romero was still in evolution, and I don't believe that he would want his words to be less timely for readers today because of antiquated use of language in the translation. I have spent a good many hours and days with Archbishop Romero—with Monseñor—over the more than twenty-five years since I began translating his diary, I have tried to be faithful to his message and his spirit and have also taken care to resist the impulse, at times, to soften his message to make it more palatable to the reader.

While I was translating the selections, I kept saying to myself that they would not be any better received in 2005 by those who didn't like what he had to say at the time (1977–1980). Two years ago, when I was asked to do a workshop on Romero and solidarity at the Mt. Notre Dame Solidarity Center in Cincinnati, I originally thought I would frame the discussion in terms of "what would Romero say to us today." As I went back through the book, I realized that it was *not* what *would* he say but rather *what he did say that we still need to hear and act on.* Reading these texts in the light of today's realities highlights unresolved societal and religious issues and a continuing need for conversion. I prepared pages of quotes on truth and how it and those who speak prophetic truth are persecuted, others in which he denounced idolatry of money, power, private property, conformity, consumerism, deformation of the Gospel; others in which he expressed concerns about pluralism, education, the environment, the right to organize, machismo, prostitution; recommended forgiveness and dialogue; discussed the importance and meaning of God's justice, honoring the martyrs, following the model of the Good Samaritan, love, speaking out in love, commitment, hope, faithfulness; decrying the opposites of hate, violence, and impunity.

I have been present at many of the Romero anniversaries since 1995 and have always been impressed by the enthusiasm and commitment of youth who hadn't even been born when Romero died. A former student asked me my opinion of an article in which Luis van de Velde questioned whether Romero would actually be "present" at his beatification since he had said that he would not attend any government functions until the death of Fr. Rutilio Grande, S.J., was properly investigated—something which has never happened. While the last two governments elected in El Salvador theoretically have been more progressive, they have not as yet been able to eliminate the great inequalities which helped to provoke the war. The article questioned also the amount of money spent on the beatification and the role of both the rich and the poor in it—whether the poor would have a voice and whether the rich would be converted. From everything I have read, as happened with the beatification of the now-sainted Alberto Hurtado of Chile, S.J., it may be that different groups are able to emphasize the parts of Romero's message that they liked and ignore, to the extent possible, the parts that prove difficult for them. Fr. Jon Sobrino, S.J., has said that he didn't want to see Romero beatified if he were to be *aguado*, watered-down, and "edulcorado," sweetened, that he wanted a beatified Romero "alive, as sharp as a double-edged sword, just and compassionate." Guillermo Cuéllar, composer of the Salvadoran folk mass, included with the Mesomerican Mass he wrote for the twentieth anniversary, the song *"Proclámenlo santo,"* "Proclaim Him a Saint." Cuéllar suggests that, although the Vatican was asking for evidence of miracles for the beatification process, the real miracle would be for them to follow Romero's example. When he was bishop of Santiago de María, Romero responded to the plight of the migrant workers sleeping in the plaza by opening church property to them. We might ask what following this example on this might mean today—and how it fits with what Pope Francis is saying about individual parishes and refugees.

I want to thank Guillermo Cuéllar and the Romero Foundation for asking me to be the translator for this important book; Bishop Ricardo Urioste and Reverend Dean Brackley, S.J., for their confidence in me and their kind words through the years about my translation of the diary; Fr. Jim Barnett, O.P., for his exuberant affirmation of this translation. I also want to thank again my students for understanding that this part of my work is essential for my classes to be life-affirming and for being patient when I was slow responding to their work as deadlines neared. I also appreciate the critical reading of different sections of the draft manuscript by members of the Board of CRISPAZ (Christians for Peace in El Salvador) in Cincinnati and Northern Kentucky, current and former members of the theology department at Xavier, staff members of Programs in Peace and Justice and Campus Ministries, both U.S. and Latin American Jesuits as well as alumni of Xavier's Academic Service Learning Semester in Nicaragua. Many of them, as a result of their experience, expressed interest in reading the entire text.

In El Salvador, I owe a debt of gratitude to Miguel Cavada, who made the original selections from the homilies as well as to Bishop Rafael Urrutia at the archdiocese canonization office and director of the Archdiocesan Press for their help in resolving questions about the original manuscript in Spanish. I was able to correct in the English translation errors in the Spanish text with their approval based on conversations and e-mails and also because of corrections that had been made in work being done for a second, corrected, edition of the homilies (which would also contain the readings of the day). Romero quoted and paraphrased saints and Bible verses off the top of his head, and the transcriptions of the homilies don't always provide the references.

We did our own research and added at the end of the first selection from each day the information for as many of the readings of the day as we could at the time so that the book would be more useful for daily meditation. To this end, we consulted both the texts of the homilies available at the time and the *Lectionary*. Joseph Hall was especially helpful with this and in tracking down biblical quotes and other references. However, it was not always possible to determine the readings for special masses, and, at times, the readings scheduled for the day didn't seem to fit with Romero's comments about the readings in a given selection.

I am grateful to Franciscan Media for their interest in Romero, publishing first the diary and then this book, especially Lisa Biedenbach and Katie Carroll for their work on the first edition and Mark Lombard and his editorial board for their willingness to publish this new edition to commemorate Romero's beatification and allow me to update my introduction and translation. I am most indebted to all the Salvadorans I have met through the years who have shared with me their stories, their faith and their love for *Monseñor* Romero. They—and he—have been a big part of why I keep doing the work that I do.

Irene B. Hodgson, Ph.D.
Xavier University
October 2004 and September 2015

WORKS CITED

Brockman, James R., S.J. *Romero: A Life* (Maryknoll, NY: Orbis, 1989).

———.*The Violence of Love* (Maryknoll, NY: Orbis, 2004).

Diaz, Zacarías and Juan Macho. *En Santiago de María me tope con la miseria: dos años de la vida de monseñor Romero: 1975-1976, años de cambio?* (San Salvador: Koinonia, 1994).

López Vigil, María. *Muerte y vida en Morazán: Testimonio de un sacerdote* [Rogelio Ponceele] (n.p.: UCA, 1987).

Metalli, Alver. "Jon Sobrino: 'Hace tiempo nos pusimos en guardia para que no beatifiquen a un monseñor Romero aguado,'" *Religion Digital*, 22 May 2015.

Sobrino, Jon, S.J. *Archbishop Romero: Memories and Reflections*. Trans. Robert R. Barr (Maryknoll, NY: Orbis, 1990).

———."Monseñor Romero: diez años de tradición," *Revista Latinoamericana de teología* (año VII: 19).

Van de Velde, Luis." ¿Estará presente monseñor Romero el 23 de mayo?" *Religión Digital*, 29 April 2015.

+

DAILY MEDITATIONS

[1] + TRUTH IS PERSECUTED

Persecution is necessary in the church. Do you know why? Because the truth is always persecuted. Jesus Christ said, "If they persecute me, they will also persecute you" [John 15:20]. And because of this, when one day they asked Pope Leo XIII, that incredibly intelligent man of the beginning of our century, what is it that sets apart the true Catholic Church, the pope said the four qualities that are already known: one, holy, catholic, and apostolic. The pope said to them, "Let's add another: persecuted." The Church that lives up to its duty cannot exist without being persecuted.

May 29, 1977

READINGS: ACTS 2:1–11; 1 CORINTHIANS 12:3B–7, 12–13;
JOHN 20:19–23

[2] + PROPHESYING

I already told you one day the simple comparison the peasant makes, "Bishop, when you stick your hand in a pan of water with salt, if the hand is whole, nothing will happen; but if there is a cut, oh, it will burn." The Church is the salt of the earth. It is to be expected that where there are wounds this salt will burn.

May 29, 1977

[3] + PLURALISM

A healthy pluralism is needed. We don't want to force everyone into the same mold. Uniformity is different from unity. Unity means pluralism, with everyone respecting how others think, and among all of us, creating a unity that is greater than just my way of thinking.

May 29, 1977

[4] + IDOLATRY

When Christ confessed that he was the Son of God, they considered this to be blasphemy and sentenced him to death. The Church continues to confess that Christ is the Lord, that there are no other gods. When human beings kneel before other gods, they are angry that the Church preaches the one God. Because of this, the Church clashes with the idols of power, with those who worship money, with those that make flesh a god, with those who think that God is unnecessary, that we don't need Christ, that the things of the world are enough. And the Church has the right and the duty to cast down all these idols and proclaim that only Christ is the Lord.

June 19, 1977

READINGS: ZECHARIAH 12:10–11; GALATIANS 3:26–29;
LUKE 9:18–24

[5] + THE GOSPEL

I think that we have greatly deformed the Gospel. We have tried to live a very comfortable Gospel, without committing ourselves, merely being pious, having a Gospel that we are content with.

June 19, 1977

[6] + FORGIVENESS

I know that it is hard to forgive after so many attacks, and, nevertheless, this is the word of the Gospel, "Love your enemies, do good to those who hate you and persecute you, be perfect as is your heavenly Father, who makes it to rain and the sun to shine on the fields of the good and of the bad" [Matthew 5:44–45]. Let there not be resentment in your hearts.

June 19, 1977

[7] + THE CHRISTIAN'S REVENGE

We shall be firm, yes, in defending our rights, but with great love in our hearts. Because by defending them in this way, with love, we are also seeking the conversion of sinners. This is the Christian's revenge.

June 19, 1977

[8] + INTERIORITY

We really live outside of ourselves. There are very few humans who truly live inside themselves and this is why there are so many problems.... In each person's heart, there is something like a small, intimate space, where God comes down to speak alone with that person. And this is where a person determines his or her own destiny, his or her own role in the world. If each of the people with so many problems were to enter at this moment this small space, and, once there, were to listen to the voice of the Lord which speaks in our own conscience, how much could each one of us do to improve the environment, society, the family with whom we live?

July 10, 1977

READINGS: DEUTERONOMY 30:10–14; COLOSSIANS 1:15–20;
LUKE 10:25–37

[9] + THE PARABLE OF THE SAMARITAN

In the parable of the Good Samaritan, we see the condemnation of everything that is intended to honor God, but which forgets about our neighbor: neither the priest, nor the Levite, nor any others who go to Mass, go to adore God, or think about God, should forget about their neighbor.

July 10, 1977

[10] + LOVE

You cannot reap what you have not sown. How are we going to reap love in our country, if we only sow hate?

July 10, 1977

[11] + COMMITMENT TO HISTORY

A Christian ought not to permit that the enemy of God, sin, reign in the world. A Christian has to work so that sin is marginalized and the kingdom of God is established. Working for this is not communism. Working for this is not getting involved in politics. It is simply the Gospel that requires of a person, of today's Christian, more commitment to history.

July 16, 1977

READINGS: ZECHARIAH 2:14–17; LUKE 2:15B–19

[12] + SIN

What is sin? Sin is the death of God. It is because of it that God died on the cross because only in that way could there be forgiveness. Sin is a violation of the law of God. It is stepping on God's plan. Sin is a lack of respect for what God wants.

July 24, 1977

READINGS: GENESIS 18:20–32; COLOSSIANS 2:12–14;

LUKE 11:1–13

[13] + CONFORMITY

People do not understand their dignity and don't work to better their situation. They live in conformity, which truly is the opiate of the people. There is a great deal of this, brothers and sisters. There are the rich who do not realize that they are guilty of social sin; also the lazy, also the marginalized that don't struggle to realize their dignity and don't work to better their lot. Everyone who is half-asleep and is lulled, such that others determine their destiny, is sinning too.

July 24, 1977

[14] + THE PROPHETIC CHURCH

The Church cannot remain silent when it sees these injustices of an economic nature, of a political nature, of a social nature. If it remains silent, the Church is complicit with those who marginalize themselves and are asleep in a conformity that is sickly and sinful, or with those who take advantage of this unawareness of the people to abuse them and corner the market politically and economically, marginalizing the immense majority of the people. This is the voice of the Church, brothers and sisters. And as long as they don't allow us the freedom to proclaim these truths of the Gospel, this is persecution. What we are talking about are substantial things, not something of little or no importance. This is a question of life or death for the kingdom of God on this earth.

July 24, 1977

[15] + PRAYER

Prayer is the peak of human development. Human beings do not have worth because of what they have, rather for what they are. And human beings really exist when they meet God face to face and understand the marvels God has done with them. God has created them intelligent beings, capable of love, free.

July 24, 1977

[16] + TRANSCENDENCE

Transcendence is a word that means the perspective on the eternal, toward God, toward the divine. Only when you look at the world, at things, at wealth, at the earth, looking toward the God who created them, do things have meaning. When we look at things, at wealth and at the riches of the earth without taking God into account, they become meaningless.

Radio message, July 31, 1977

READINGS: ECCLESIASTES 1:2, 2:21–23; COLOSSIANS 3:1–5, 9–11; LUKE 12:13–21

[17] + IMPUNITY

There is no crime that will remain unpunished. He who lives by the sword, dies by the sword, the Bible says. All of these abuses of power in this country will not go unpunished.

August 7, 1977

READINGS: WISDOM 18:6–9; HEBREWS 11:1–2, 8–9; LUKE 12:32–48

[18] + GOD

God does not walk over there, through puddles of blood and torture. God walks on clean paths of hope and love.

August 7, 1977

[19] + SOCIAL SANCTION

There used to be social sanctions. They say that the people who went to a casino had such a strong sense of their own nobility that, if a murderer or a thief came in, even though he was apparently a great man, they would not shake hands with him, because offering him their hand was a sign that they were in complete agreement with him. I wish this noble sense of social sanction would be resurrected and we would reproach all those who are not in accord with God's projects, respecting their right to their own way of thinking, but knowing that this is not building true peace.

August 14, 1977
READINGS: JEREMIAH 38:4–6, 8–10; HEBREWS 12:1–4;
LUKE 12:49–53

[20] + A PROPHET

A prophet has to be angry with society, when that society is not in accord with God.

August 14, 1977

[21] + MY LIFE DOESN'T BELONG TO ME

Among the events of this week, which, of course, are many, one stands out for me with a sense of gratitude, the celebration of my birthday, through which I have understood once again that my life doesn't belong to me, but to all of you.

August 21, 1977
READINGS: ISAIAH 66:18–21; HEBREWS 12:5–7, 11–13;
LUKE 13:22–30

[22] + CONVERSION

If you live out a Christianity that is good but that is not sufficient for our times, that doesn't denounce injustice, that doesn't proclaim the kingdom of God courageously, that doesn't reject the sins humankind commits, that consents to the sins of certain classes so as to be accepted by those classes, then you are not doing your duty, you are sinning, you are betraying your mission. The Church was put here to convert humankind, not to tell people that everything that they do is all right; and, because of that, naturally, it irritates people. Everything that corrects us irritates us. I know that I have irritated many people, but I know that I am well liked by all those who work sincerely for the conversion of the church.

August 21, 1977

[23] + THE VOICE OF THE VOICELESS

We want to be the voice of the voiceless, to cry out against so many violations of human rights. Let justice be done, let there not be so many criminals staining the fabric of the country, of the army. Let us recognize who the criminals are and give just recompense to the families left unprotected.

August 28, 1977

READINGS: ECCLESIASTES 3:19–21, 30–31;
HEBREWS 12:18–19, 22–24A; LUKE 14:1, 7–14

[24] + JESUS, THE ONLY LEADER

I have never believed myself to be the leader of a people, because there is only one leader: Jesus Christ. Jesus is the fountain of hope. I base what I preach on Jesus. In Jesus is the truth of what I am saying.

August 28, 1977

[25] + THE POOR CHURCH

The Church today does not rely on any power, on wealth. Today the Church is poor. Today the Church knows that the powerful reject her, but that she is loved by those who put their faith in God.... This is the Church that I want. A Church that does not rely on the privileges and the worth of earthly things. A Church ever more detached from earthly things, human things, so that she can judge them more freely from her perspective of the Gospel, from her poverty.

August 28, 1977

[26] + IDOLATRY OF WEALTH

What else is wealth when you do not take God into account? It is a golden idol, a golden calf. They adore it, bow down before it and make sacrifices to it. What enormous sacrifices are made out of idolatry of money! Not just sacrifices, but injustices. People are paid to kill. People are paid to sin. And they sell themselves. Everything is commercialized. Everything is licit for money.

September 11, 1977

READINGS: EXODUS 32:7–11, 13–14;

TIMOTHY 1:12–17; LUKE 15:1–32

[27] + THE CHURCH OF THE POOR

When the Church is called the church of the poor, it is not because it consents to this sinful poverty. The Church draws near the poor sinners to tell them: Be converted, improve your situation, don't be lulled into sleep. And this mission to improve people's situation, that the Church is carrying out, is also bothersome. Because many prefer to have the masses asleep, to be people who are not awake, people who conform, who are satisfied with the nuts fed to the pigs. The Church does not accept this sinful poverty. Yes, it wants a poverty that is dignified, a poverty that is the result of injustice and the struggle to free oneself from it; the dignified poverty of a home in Nazareth. Mary and Joseph were poor, but what a saintly poverty, what a dignified poverty. Thank God that we also have this kind of poor among us. And from this category of the dignified poor, of poor saints, Christ proclaims: Blessed are those who hunger, blessed are those who weep, blessed are those who thirst for justice. The Church cries out from that same place, following the example of Christ, that this is the poverty that will save the world. Because both the rich and the poor have to become poor, in an evangelical sense, not the poverty that is the fruit of disorder and vice; but rather the poverty that has freed itself, that is trusting that everything will come from God, that is turning its back on the golden calf in order to adore the one God, that is sharing the happiness of having with those who have not, that is the joy of loving.

September 11, 1977

[28] + LOVE OF GOD AND OF YOUR NEIGHBOR

These unjust inequalities, these masses living in misery who cry out to heaven are a sign of our anti-Christianity. They are declaring before God that we believe more in the things of the earth than in the covenant of love that we have signed with him, and that because of our covenant with God, all human beings should consider themselves brothers and sisters.... Human beings are more children of God when they become more brotherly or sisterly to other human beings, and less children of God when they feel less kinship with their neighbors.

September 18, 1977

READINGS: AMOS 8:4–7; I TIMOTHY 2:1–8; LUKE 16:1–13

[29] + AMONG THE PEOPLE

It is true that I have been to El Jicarón, to El Salitre, and many other small villages; I glory in being among my people and feeling the affection of all of these people who see in the Church, through their bishop, hope.

September 25, 1977

READINGS: AMOS 6:1A, 4–7; I TIMOTHY 6, 11–16; LUKE 16, 19–31

[30] + ACCORDING TO GOD'S HEART

Their hearts don't want to hear even if someone would come back from the dead to tell them: We are in a bad way in El Salvador. This ugly image of our country should not be made–up to look pretty from outside. We have to make it pretty here inside so that it can be pretty outside too. But, as long as there are mothers who are crying about the disappearance of their sons and daughters, as long as there are tortures in the headquarters of our security forces, as long as there are sybaritic abuses of private property, as long as there is horrible disorder, brothers and sisters, there cannot be peace, and there will continue to be acts of violence and bloodshed. Repression doesn't resolve anything. We need to be rational and listen to the voice of God, to organize a more just society, one more according to God's heart. Anything else is merely putting a Band-Aid on the problem. The names of those murdered may change, but there will always be people murdered. The violence may have a different name, but there will always be violence as long as the root of all these things that are so horrible in our atmosphere remains unchanged.

September 25, 1977

[31] + NO ONE CAN MOCK GOD

No one can mock God. His law will prevail forever. And this God, that is love for us, turns into justice when we haven't known how to respond to the invitation of love.... God will wait, but when God loses patience with love, his justice begins. Brothers and sisters, it is not a return to the Middle Ages to speak of hell. It is looking face-to-face at God's justice, which no one can mock. Let's organize our country while there is still time. Let's organize the riches that God has given us for the happiness of all Salvadorans. Let's make this republic a beautiful entryway to the Lord's paradise, and we will have the blessing of being received like poor Lazarus.

September 25, 1977

[32] + FROM THE PEOPLE FAITHFUL TO THE WILL OF GOD

I am receiving many anonymous messages that are really crude. Brothers and sisters, know that the position that I have taken is out of conscience. It is not just the result of pressure as some say; it is simply the duty of a pastor who feels the joy, and at the same time the anguish, of living with his people. And, from this people, faithful to the will of God, to follow a path that would be truly that of the Lord.

October 9, 1977

READINGS: 2 KINGS 5:14–17; 2 TIMOTHY 2:8–13; LUKE 17:11–19

[33] + CONSEQUENCES OF SIN

The bishops said in Medellín that the masses living in misery are a sin, an injustice that cries out to heaven. Marginalization, hunger, illiteracy, malnutrition, and so many other miseries that penetrate the pores of our being, are consequences of sin. They are consequences of the sin of those who amass everything for themselves and share nothing with others. It is also the sin of those who, having nothing, don't struggle to improve their lot; those who conform or are lazy, who don't struggle for their own betterment. But many times they don't struggle, not through any fault of their own; it is because of their conditioning and because there are structures that don't allow them to make any progress. It is a combination, then, of sin on both sides.

October 9, 1977

[34] + WITH A BIG HEART

I am hurt by the lie when they say that I want to be the bishop of just one social class and that I despise the other class. Not so, brothers and sisters. I try to have a heart that is as big as that of Christ, to imitate him in something that calls all of us to this saving word, so that all of us might be converted, myself first, all of us converted to this word that exhorts, inspires and raises us up.

October 16, 1977

READINGS: EXODUS 17:8–13; 2 TIMOTHY 3:14 – 4:2; LUKE 18:1–8

[35] + THE EVIL IS VERY PROFOUND

The evil is very profound in El Salvador, and if there is not an all-out effort to cure it, we will always be (as we have said) calling it by different names, but it is always the same evil.

October 23, 1977

READINGS: ISAIAH 60:1–6; ROMANS 10:9–18; MATTHEW 28:16–20

[36] + THE BIBLE AND THE SIGNS OF THE TIMES

Besides reading the Bible, which is the word of God, a Christian who is faithful to the word must also read the signs of the times, the events, to illuminate them through the word.

October 30, 1977

READINGS: WISDOM 11:22—12:2; 2 THESSALONIANS 1:11—2:2;

LUKE 19:1–10

[37] + THE BISHOP

The shepherd must be where the suffering is.

October 30, 1977

[38] + THE CATECHIST MARTYRS

I want to remember our dear brother and sister catechists. It would be impossible to list them all: but, let's remember, for example, Filomena Puertas, Miguel Martínez, and so many others, dear brothers and sisters, who have worked, who have died, and who in the hour of their pain, of their painful agony, while the skin was pulled off their bodies, while they were tortured and gave their lives, while they were riddled with bullets, rose to heaven. Are they victorious there? Who has won? Like the Psalmist, we can ask those who killed them and those who continue to persecute Christians: Oh, death, where is thy victory? The victory belongs to faith. Those who have been killed in the name of justice are the ones who are victorious.

October 30, 1977

[39] + BLESSED ARE THE LIBERATORS

Blessed are the liberators who put their strength not in weapons, not in kidnapping, not in violence, nor in money, but rather know that liberation must come from God; it will be the wonderful coming together of the liberating power of God and the Christian effort of human beings.

October 30, 1977

[40] + WE ARE ONLY CHRISTIANS

Don't fear conservatives, especially all those who don't want you to talk about social issues, about thorny topics, in the way the world needs today. Don't be afraid that those of us who talk about these things have become Communists or subversives. We are only Christians, taking from the Gospel the consequences that today, at this time, humankind, our people, need.

October 30, 1977

[41] + DOING THE WILL OF GOD

The destiny of a person is not to have a great deal of money, to have great power, to be very visible, but rather to know how to do the will of God.

November 6, 1977
READINGS: 2 MACCABEES 7:1–2, 9–14;
2 THESSALONIANS 2:15 – 3:5; LUKE 20:27–38

[42] + THE THEOLOGY OF MARTYRDOM

Read chapter 7 of the second book of Maccabees. There you will find a theology of martyrdom. A theology that our people really need today. The theology of witness of faithfulness to the law of God rather than obeying those who profane the law of the Lord, the rights of the Lord. Taking together the responses of the seven children—or offspring, some were older—we conclude that Israel's thinking lacked these ideas: we have to obey God's law even at the risk of dying.

November 6, 1977

[43] + CHRISTIANITY

Christianity is not a collection of truths that one has to believe, of laws one has to keep, a list of prohibitions. That would be repugnant. Christianity is a person that loved me so much that he demands my love. Christianity is Christ.

November 6, 1977

[44] + THE LANGUAGE OF HOPE

Yesterday I heard over at Santiago de María that, according to some of my friends, I have changed, that I now preach revolution, hate, class struggle, that I am a Communist. You all know what language I use for preaching. It is a language that wants to plant seeds of hope; yes, it denounces earthly injustices, abuses of power, but not with hatred, rather with love, calling for conversion.

November 6, 1977

[45] + VIOLENCE

There are two kinds of violence: that which oppresses from above, politically and economically, and another which reacts against that violence. "These two aspects," the Vatican goes on to say, "can be difficult to separate, and the injustice can be reciprocal." There can be injustice in both kinds. "Evidently," these are the Vatican's words, "there is injustice in the first violence." That is, here the document of the Holy See calls the situation of repression, of wanting to have more, of wanting to be powerful even if it means oppressing the weak, unjust. "Evidently in the first case this is true, but also frequently in the second." I am never going to defend, nor can anyone Catholic defend, unjust violence, even when it comes from the most oppressed. It will always be unjust if it goes beyond the limits of God's law.

November 13, 1977

[Note: Romero is quoting from a Vatican bulletin announcing the theme for 1978, "No to violence, yes to peace."]

READINGS: MALACHI 4:1–2A;
2 THESSALONIANS 3:7–12; LUKE 21:5–19

[46] + I AM VERY HAPPY TO BELONG TO THIS CHURCH

I am very happy to belong to this Church that is awakening the consciousness of the peasant, of the worker, not to make them subversive—we have already said that sinful violence is not good—but rather so that they know how to be the subjects of their own destiny, so they not be merely part of a dormant mass, so together they are men and women who know how to think, who know how to make demands. This is the glory of the Church, and we should in no way be ashamed when they want to confuse it with other ideologies, because it is apparent that this is calumny and is intended to blow smoke and to discredit this kind of promotion on the part of the Church.

November 13, 1977

[47] + THE TOUCHSTONE

Brothers and sisters, do you want to know if your Christianity is real? Here is the touchstone. With whom do you get along well? Who are critical of you? Who don't accept you? Who flatter you? We know that at one point Christ said: I have not come to bring peace but rather strife, and there will be division even within the same family, because some want to live in greater comfort, following the norms of the world and of money, while others, on the other hand, have understood the call of Christ and have to reject everything that isn't just in the world.

November 13, 1977

[48] + DIALOGUE

Brothers and sisters, dialogue can't be characterized by defending one's own point of view. Dialogue is characterized by poverty: becoming poor to seek with another the truth, the solution. If both parties to a conflict go only to defend their positions, they will leave in the same condition in which they arrived.

November 20, 1977

READINGS: 2 SAMUEL 5:1–3; COLOSSIANS 1:12–20; LUKE 23:35–43

[49] + THE PERSECUTED CHURCH

Brothers and sisters, we ought not to think it strange when there is talk of a persecuted Church. Many are scandalized and say that we are exaggerating, that there is no persecuted Church. But this is the historical role of the Church! It always should be persecuted. A doctrine which goes against immorality, that preaches against abuses, that always preaches good and attacks evil, is a doctrine given by Christ to sanctify hearts, redeem societies. And, naturally, when in this society or in this heart, there is sin, there is selfishness, there is corruption of power, there is envy, there is avarice, well, then, sin jumps up like a serpent when we try to stomp on it, and persecutes the one who tries to pursue evil, sin. For this reason, when the Church is persecuted, it is a sign that it is carrying out its mission.

November 25, 1977

[50] + THE FLATTERY OF THE PERSECUTOR

First, persecution tries to flatter, to tame; and if you bow to this flattery, then there is no need for persecution, you are already defeated. Because of this, be very careful, brothers and sisters, don't let yourselves be flattered. When flattery comes from sin, and when it has to do with not getting upset, with not sacrificing oneself, with being well off, with establishing oneself in comfort on this planet, this is bad, because then you have also become a persecutor.

November 25, 1977

[51] + THE POWER OF THE WORD

The Word is power. The Word, when it is not a lie, carries the power of truth. For this reason, there are so many words that no longer have any power in our country because they are lying words, because they are words that no longer have any reason to exist.

November 25, 1977

[52] + LIBERATION

The word that bothers many, liberation, is a reality of the redemption of Christ. Liberation means the redemption of humankind, not only after death such that they are told to "resign yourselves in this life." No, liberation means that there is no exploitation in this world of human beings by other human beings. Liberation means redemption that wants to free humankind from so many kinds of slavery: the slavery of illiteracy; the slavery of being hungry because of not having enough to buy food; the slavery of not having a roof over your head, of not having anywhere to live. Slavery, misery, all of this goes together.

November 25, 1977

[53] + THE BIBLE AND HISTORICAL REALITY

We can't separate the Word of God from the historical reality in which it was spoken, because then it would no longer be the Word of God, it would be history, a pious book, a Bible that belongs in a library. But it truly becomes the Word of God because it inspires, it illuminates, it provides contrast, it rejects, it praises what is being done today in our society.

November 27, 1977

READINGS: ISAIAH 2:1–5; ROMANS 13:11–14; MATTHEW 24:37–44

[54] + INSTRUMENT OF POWER

A Gospel that doesn't take into account the rights of human beings, a Christianity that doesn't make a positive contribution to the history of the world, is not the authentic doctrine of Christ, but rather simply an instrument of power. We regret that at some moments our Church has also fallen into this sin; but we want to change this attitude and, according to this spirituality that is authentically of the Gospel, we don't want to be a plaything of the worldly powers, rather we want to be the Church that carries the authentic, courageous Gospel of our Lord Jesus Christ, even when it might become necessary to die like he did, on a cross.

November 27, 1977

[55] + A STRONG CRY AGAINST INJUSTICE

My conscience is clear, for I have never incited anyone to violence. All those paid ads [in the newspapers*] and lies and those voices on the radio screaming against the revolutionary bishop are slander, because my voice has never been tainted by a cry of resentment nor of rancor. It is a strong cry against injustice, but a cry that says to the unjust: Be converted! I cry out in the name of those in pain to say to the criminals: Be converted! Don't be evil!*

December 1, 1977

[56] + MARY, SYMBOL OF THE OPPRESSED PEOPLE

Mary, brothers and sisters, is the symbol of the people that suffer oppression, injustice, because she represents the serene sorrow that waits for the resurrection. She is Christian pain, the pain of the Church that is not in agreement with the present injustice, but with no resentment, waiting for the moment when the Resurrected One will return to give us the awaited redemption.

December 1, 1977

---

* In Salvadoran newspapers, people can pay to place an article, called a "campo pagado." These are often difficult to distinguish from news articles written by the newspaper.

[57] + THE CHURCH IS NOT FLEETING

Brothers and sisters, the Church is not fleeting. The Church waits confidently for the moment of redemption. Those who have disappeared will once again appear. The grief of these mothers will become Easter. The anguish of this people that doesn't know where it is heading, amid so much anguish, will be the Easter of resurrection if we join together with Christ, if we trust in him.

December 1, 1977

[58] + IF WE ARE TALKING ABOUT FARAWAY GALAXIES

It is often asked, "Why is it that in such and such a church, in such and such a place, there aren't any problems?" There aren't any problems if we are talking about faraway galaxies, if we are talking about the things that don't have anything to do with problems that tax our patience, our strength, and our contemporary commitment to history.

December 4, 1977

READINGS: ISAIAH 11:1–10; ROMANS 15:4–9; MATTHEW 3:1–12

[59] + THE WORD IS LIKE A RAY OF SUNSHINE

The Word of God, according to St. Paul, has to be a Word that springs from the eternal ancient Word of God but that touches the present wound, today's injustices, today's abuses, and this is what causes problems. This is to say, "The Church is getting involved in politics, the Church is becoming Communist." This accusation is really getting old! Understand once and for all: it is not sticking its nose in politics, rather it is the word like a ray of sunshine that comes from above and lights the way. What fault does the sun have that its light, its pure light, finds puddles, manure, and trash on the earth? It has to shine light on it, if not, it would not be the sun. It would not be light if it didn't show what is ugly, what is horrible that exists on earth, in the same way that it shines light on the beauty of the flowers and shows the enchantment of nature. The Word of God also, brothers and sisters, on the one hand shines light on what is horrible, ugly, and unjust on earth and inspires the good heart, the hearts that, thank God, abound.

December 4, 1977

[60] + RELIGION OF SUNDAY MASS BUT OF UNJUST WEEKDAYS

Good works, Christian hearts, true justice, charity, this is what God looks for in religion. A religion which means going to Mass on Sunday but committing injustices the rest of the week is not pleasing to the Lord. A religion which involves a great deal of prayer but with a hypocritical heart is not Christian. A Church that accommodates itself to be comfortable, to have a great deal of wealth, great comfort, but that ignores the clamor against injustice, would not be the true Church of our divine Savior.

December 4, 1977

[61] + MY SOUL IS SORE

My soul is sore when I learn how our people are tortured, when I learn how the rights of those created in the image of God are violated. This should not happen. Human beings without God are wild beasts. Human beings without God are a desert. Their hearts do not have flowers of love, their hearts are perverted and they persecute their brothers and sisters.

December 5, 1977

[62] + A WORD WITHOUT COMMITMENT

Dear brothers and sisters, let not your service be false to the Word of God. It is very easy to serve the word without making the world uncomfortable. A Word that is very spiritual, a Word with no commitment to history, a Word that can be heard in any part of the world because it doesn't belong anywhere; this kind of Word doesn't cause problems, doesn't give rise to conflicts. What gives rise to conflicts, to persecution, what characterizes the true Church, is when the burning Word, like that of the prophets, announces to the people and announces the marvels of God so that people believe and adore him, and denounces the sins of humankind, that are opposed to the kingdom of God, so that they are torn from their hearts, from their societies, from their laws, from their organizations that oppress, that imprison, that violate the rights of God and of human beings.

December 10, 1977

[63] + COSMIC LIBERATION

The liberation that the Church awaits is a cosmic liberation. The Church feels that all of nature is moaning under the weight of sin. What beautiful coffee fields, what beautiful cane fields, what beautiful cotton fields, what farms! God has given us all this! How beautiful nature is! But when we see her moan under oppression, under wrongdoing, under injustice, under abuse, then the Church aches and awaits a liberation that is not only one of material wellbeing, but rather one of the power of God that will free nature from the sinful hands of humankind so that, together with the redeemed humans, it will sing of happiness in the liberator God.

December 11, 1977

READINGS: ISAIAH 35:1–6A, 10; JAMES 5:7–10; MATTHEW 11:2–11

[64] + DON'T MEASURE WORTH BY COUNTING HOW MANY ARE IN THE CROWD

Brothers and sisters, we don't measure the Church by the number of people, nor do we measure the Church by its material buildings. The Church has built many temples, many seminaries, many buildings. The material walls stay, become part of history. What matters are all of you, the men and women, the hearts, the grace of God giving you truth and the life of God. Don't measure worth by counting how many are in the crowd, count the sincerity of the heart with which they follow this truth and the grace of our Divine Savior.

December 19, 1977

[65] + LOVE YOUR COUNTRY

Salvadorans, the Virgin calls us to be like her: Love your country, study your history, know your idiosyncrasies, be fully Salvadoran. Perhaps we are not fully to blame if we don't love our country as deeply as Mary loved her country. We see its ugliness, we feel so displaced in our own country that many prefer to leave it and go somewhere else. They don't feel at home, they don't feel the traditions are theirs, they don't feel the joy of their own blood, of their countryside, of the beauty of their land itself. And El Salvador is so beautiful!

January 1, 1978

READINGS: NUMBERS 6:22–27; GALATIANS 4:4–7; LUKE 2:16–21

[66] + GOD WANTS TO SAVE US AS A PEOPLE

God wants to save us as a whole people. He does not want an isolated salvation. Because of this, today's Church, more than ever, is emphasizing the sense of being one people. And this is why the Church is having conflicts. Because the Church doesn't want a mass of people, it wants a united people. A mass is a crowd of people the more asleep, the better; the more they conform, the better. The Church wants to wake men and women up to the true sense of being one people. What is a people? A people is a community of men and women in which everyone works together for the common good.

January 5, 1978

READINGS: ISAIAH 42:1–4, 6–7; ACTS 10:34–38; MATTHEW 3:13–17

[67] + PREACHING THAT DOES NOT DENOUNCE

Preaching that does not denounce sin is not preaching from the Gospel. Preaching that keeps sinners happy so that they stay rooted in their situations of sin is betraying the call of the Gospel. Preaching that does not bother the sinner but rather lulls him in his sin is leaving Zebulon and Naphtali in their shadow of sin. Preaching that awakens, preaching that illuminates, like when a light comes on and someone is asleep, naturally it will bother them, but it has awakened them. This is the preaching of Christ: awaken, be converted. This is the authentic preaching of the Church. Naturally, brothers and sisters, this kind of preaching will generate conflict, it will lose a false prestige, it will bother people, it will be persecuted. It can't be in harmony with the power of shadows and of sin.

January 22, *1978*

READINGS: ISAIAH 9:1–4; 1 CORINTHIANS 1:10–13, 17;

MATTHEW 4:12–23

[68] + THOSE DEVOTED TO JUSTICE

Each one of us has to have a burning commitment to justice, to human rights, to freedom, to equality, but looking at them with the light of faith. It's not doing good out of philanthropy. There are many groups that do good, but so that they will be in the newspaper, so that there will be a plaque with their names as great benefactors. There are many who do good looking for recognition on earth. What the Church is looking for is to call all of us to do justice and to brotherly and sisterly love. This is for the benefit of the person who does good, because the benefactor receives more good than the one to whom good is done. "Then you will call out to the Lord and he will answer you; you will cry out and he will say: Here I am" [Isaiah 58:9]. What more can we want, brothers and sisters?

February 5, 1978
READINGS: ISAIAH 58:7–10; CORINTHIANS 2:1–5;
MATTHEW 5:13–16

[69] + RELIGION IS NOT PRAYING A GREAT DEAL

There is a way to know if God is near us or far away: Everyone who is concerned about the hungry, about the naked, about the poor, about the disappeared, about the tortured, about the prisoner, about all the flesh that is suffering, will find God near. "Call out to the Lord and he will hear you." Religion is not praying a great deal. Religion involves this promise of having my God near because I do good to my brothers and sisters. My devotion is not shown by saying a great many words; the devotion in my prayers is easy to see: How do I treat the poor? Because that's where God is.

February 5, 1978

[70] + CHRISTIANS WHO ARE NOT COMMITTED

History is so dense in El Salvador, dear brothers and sisters, that it is never-ending. Each Sunday we find events that need the light of the word of God. And the true Christians in El Salvador cannot overlook these realities, unless they want an unearthly Christianity, without reality on earth, a Christianity without commitment, spiritualism. And it is very easy to be that kind of Christian, unembodied, not paying attention to the realities of life. But, living in this Gospel of Christ, that by order of the eternal Father we have to listen to: Christ, "Listen to him" [Matthew 17:5b], living it in the actual circumstances of our existence. This is the hard way, this is what causes conflict, but it is what makes the preaching of the Gospel and the life of the Christian authentic.

February 19, 1978
READINGS: GENESIS 12:1–4A; 2 TIMOTHY 1:8B–10;
MATTHEW 17:1–9

[71] + NO TO VIOLENCE

It scares me, brothers and sisters, when repressive laws or violent attitudes are denying the legitimate avenues [of expression] of a people that needs to be able to protest. What happens with the kettle that is boiling and has no escape valve? It can explode. There is still time to let our people express themselves as they wish. As long as, at the same time, justice rules. Because naturally, brothers and sisters, when we defend these just aspirations we are not taking the side of terrorist demands. The Church does not agree with any kind of violence, not that which springs forth as the fruit of repression, nor that which oppresses in such barbarous ways. It simply calls for understanding one another, for dialogue, for justice, for love.

March 19, 1978
READINGS: ISAIAH 50:4–7; PHILIPPIANS 2:6–11;
MATTHEW 26:14–27:66

[72] + THE CRUCIFIED PEOPLE

We sense in the Christ of Holy Week, carrying his cross, that the people are also carrying their cross. We sense in the Christ with open and crucified arms the crucified people; but a people that, crucified and humiliated, receives its hope from Christ.

March 19, 1978

[73] + NOT KNOWING HOW TO LOVE

This is the great sickness of today's world: not knowing how to love. Everything is selfishness, everything is the exploitation of human beings by other human beings, everything is cruelty, torture. Everything is repression, violence. They burn the houses of their brothers and sisters, they take their brothers and sisters prisoner and torture them. There are so many horrible acts of one person against another! How Jesus would suffer tonight to see the atmosphere in our country of so many crimes and so much cruelty! I seem to see Christ saddened looking at El Salvador from his Passover table and saying: and I told them to love one another like I loved them.

March 23, 1978

READINGS: EXODUS 12:1–8, 11–14; 1 CORINTHIANS 11:23–26; JOHN 13:1–15

[74] + THE VICTORY OF CHRIST

Victories that are amassed through blood are hateful. Victories that are achieved by brute force are beastly. The victory that triumphs is that of faith. It is the victory of Christ, who didn't come to be served but rather to serve.

March 25, 1978

READINGS: GENESIS 1:1–2:2; 22:1–18; EXODUS 14:15–15:1; ISAIAH 54:5–14; 55:1–11; BARUCH 3:9–15, 32–44; EZEKIEL 36:16–28; ROMANS 6:3–11; MATTHEW 28:1–10

[75] + THE CHURCH CANNOT BE DEAF OR DUMB

The Church cannot be deaf or dumb faced with the clamor of millions of men and women who shout for freedom, oppressed by a thousand slaveries. But it tells them what is the true freedom that they should strive for: the one that Christ already inaugurated on earth when he was resurrected and broke the chains of sin, of death and of hell. Being like Christ, free from sin, is to be truly free with the true liberation. And those who, with their faith placed in the Resurrected One, work for a more just world, against the abuses of a repressive authority, against the disorder of human beings exploiting other human beings, those who struggle based on the resurrection of the Great Liberator, only they are authentic Christians.

March 26, 1978

READINGS: ACTS 10:34A, 37–43; COLOSSIANS 3:1–4; JOHN 20:1–9

[76] + THE CHRISTIAN COMMITMENT

Brothers and sisters, the parable of Christ condemned the attitude of a priest and of a Levite because it is not enough to wear a religious habit or to say that I am a Catholic to gain God's approval. Charity is above all love of neighbor. And, even though one is a bishop or a priest or has been baptized, if that person doesn't follow the example of the Good Samaritan, if, like the bad priests of the old law, he goes a roundabout way so as to not encounter the wounded body, not touch such things, "be prudent, let's not offend anybody, more gently," then, brothers and sisters, we are not carrying out what God commanded: We are going a roundabout way. How many go a roundabout way so as to not confront themselves! And, the more they go a roundabout way, the more they meet up with themselves, because they carry with them their own conscience which will not allow them to be at peace as long as they don't face the situation. The Christian commitment is very serious. And, above all, our commitment as priests and bishops obliges us to go out and meet the poor wounded person on the road.

April 2, 1978
READINGS: ACTS 2:42–47; 1 PETER 1:3–9; JOHN 20:19–31

[77] + THE MEDIA

It is a shame, brothers and sisters, that in these matters of our people that are so grave, they want to deceive the people. It is a shame that we have media that has sold out. It is a shame that we can't trust the news in the newspaper or on television or on the radio because it has all been bought, it has been tamed. And it doesn't tell the truth.

April 2, 1978

[78] + WE OUGHT TO SERVE THE POOR MAJORITY

We are issuing a call for reason and reflection. Our country cannot go on this way. We have to overcome the indifference of many who are sitting back as spectators watching the terrible situation, especially in the countryside. We must struggle against the selfishness that is hidden in those who don't want to give up what they have so that it might go further. We have to again find the deep evangelical truth that we must serve the poor majority.

April 2, 1978

[79] + TO SERVE IS TO SACRIFICE YOURSELF

You all know that, given the situation, I have organized a solidarity committee. Because of a generous initiative from a fine lady, a call went out to all the organizations that we could think of. Many came, but many others only sent a message, "We can't, because we can't take sides." Another, "Because we can't get involved in politics." What a shame, brothers and sisters, that we can be so cold using the excuse of not getting involved in politics! You sit back with your arms folded and do good only when doing good is easy or will bring glory, bring prestige. To serve is to make sacrifices.

April 2, 1978

[80] + YOU ARE THE ONES WHO HAVE TO MAKE YOUR POSITION CLEAR

In case there is a Catholic that is uncertain about what the bishop means and is going around saying loudly, "Let the bishop make his position clear": I have made my position clear, brothers and sisters! You are the ones who have to make your position clear.

April 2, 1978

[81] + WHAT KIND OF GOSPEL IS THAT?

This is what the Church wants: to bother your conscience, to provoke a crisis in the times we are living in. A Church that doesn't stir up a crisis, a Gospel that doesn't make us uncomfortable, a Word of God that—to put it crudely—doesn't cause an allergic rash, a Word of God that doesn't touch on the specific sins of the society in which it is spoken, what kind of Gospel is that? Very beautiful pious concerns that won't bother anyone is how many want the sermons to be. And those preachers who, so as not to bother anyone and so as not to have conflicts and difficulties, do not shed light on the reality they are living in, lack the courage of Peter to say to the mob, which still has the blood-stained hands that killed Christ, "You killed him!" [Acts 2:23]. Although he would also lose his life because of this accusation, he proclaimed it. It is the courageous Gospel; it is the Good News that came to take away the sins of the world.

April 16, 1978

READINGS: ACTS 2:14A, 36–41; PETER 2:20B–25; JOHN 10:1–10

[82] + LET THIS BE PERFECTLY CLEAR

Let this be perfectly clear, because the Church cannot identify itself with any political party nor with any organization of a political, social, or cooperative nature. The Church doesn't have a system. The Church doesn't have methodologies. The Church only has Christian inspiration, an obligation to charity that urges it to accompany those who suffer injustice and also to help achieve just demands.

April 16, 1978

[83] + HOW DIABOLIC THIS SYSTEM HAS HAD TO BE!

And one of the greatest sins that hurts me so is this, brothers and sisters: the current system of our country has come to a situation of confrontation with the peasants. The same hunger that ravishes a person from the BLOQUE is the same hunger that also affects a member of ORDEN. We have to remember that the agents of our army have also come from the peasants. And when I see police watching peasants, peasants watching peasants, ORDEN in confrontation with the BLOQUE, I say: How diabolic this system has had to be to manage to take advantage of people's hunger, their need to earn a living, even if it be by persecuting, becoming enemies, becoming divided, when they were in the same poverty!

April 16, 1978

[*Note:* BLOQUE refers to the Bloque Popular Revolucionario, the Popular Revolutionary Bloc, a coalition of popular organizations; ORDEN refers to the Organización Democrática Nacionalista, the Democratic Nationalist Organization, the government's antisubversive paramilitary organization, composed primarily of peasants, which operated in rural areas.]

[84] + WE BISHOPS DON'T GIVE ORDERS AS IF WE WERE DESPOTS

We bishops don't give orders as if we were despots. It shouldn't be that way. The bishop is the most humble servant of the community because Christ told the apostles, the first bishops, "The one who wants to be greatest among you, become the least, be the servant of all" [Mark 10:43]. Our mandate is service. Our behavior, our word, is service.

April 23, 1978

READINGS: ACTS 6:1–7; 1 PETER 2:4–9; JOHN 14:1–12

[85] + THEY ARE VICTIMS OF THE GOD MOLOCH

This week we are also mourning the deaths of two policemen. They are our brothers. When faced with abuses and violence, I have never lent my voice to one side. I have placed myself, with the compassion of Christ, on the side of the dead, of those who suffer, and I have asked that we pray for them, and that we unite in the solidarity of grief with their families. I have said that the two policemen who have died are two more victims of the injustice of our system that, as I denounced last week, has among its greatest crimes provoking confrontation with our poor. Police and workers and peasants belong to the poor class. It is an evil system that provokes the confrontation of the poor against each other. Two dead policemen are two poor men who have been victims of others who are perhaps also poor, and who, in any case, are victims of the god Moloch, who, insatiable for power, as long as he maintains his unjust systems doesn't care about the lives of the peasants, nor of the police, nor of the Guardia, but rather fights to defend a system that is very sinful.

April 30, 1978

[*Note:* Guardia refers to the Guardia Nacional, the National Guard, a largely volunteer force used for internal security.]

READINGS: ACTS 8:5–8, 14–17; 1 PETER 3:15–18; JOHN 14:15–21

[86] + EDUCATION FOR POLITICAL PARTICIPATION

Let children and young people be trained to analyze the realities of their country. Let them be prepared to be agents of change, instead of alienating them with a mountain of textbooks and techniques that keep them from knowing reality. There are many technicians like that, many wise people, many professionals who know their science, their profession, but are like angels, disconnected from the reality in which they practice their profession. The first thing education should seek is to locate human beings in reality, so that they know how to analyze it, how to be critical of their reality. This means an education that is education for political participation that is democratic and conscious. How much good this could do!

April 30, 1978

[87] + IT'S BETTER TO BE FREE IN THE TRUTH

It's a shame that so many who earn their daily bread from the radio have sold their pens and so many their tongues, and feed themselves through lying since that is what pays! Truth many times doesn't result in money but rather in a bitter harvest. But it is better to be free in the truth than to earn a great deal of money through lies.

May 7, 1978

READINGS: ACTS 1:1–11; EPHESIANS 1:17–23; MATTHEW 28:16–20

[88] + I AM WILLING TO FACE TRIAL AND JAIL

My denouncing is inspired in a positive *"animus corrigenda"* [a "spirit of correction"] and not in an evil spirit of criticizing. I think that it is my duty to denounce in my role as shepherd of a people suffering injustice. I am required to do this by the Gospel, for which I am willing to face trial and jail, even though that would only be adding on another injustice.

May 14, 1978

READINGS: ACTS 2:1–11; 1 CORINTHIANS 12:3B–7, 12–13;
JOHN 20:19–23

[89] + SADLY, WE LIVE IN AN ATHEIST SOCIETY

A people, a person, in whom the tenderness of God has dissipated, who prefers that God not exist so they can commit injustices, and commits sin that God will punish, provides the impetus for a practical atheism. This means that not only Marxism is atheist, for capitalism is also practical atheism. It makes a god of money, idolizes power, raises false idols to substitute for the true God. Sadly, we live in an atheist society.

May 21, 1978

READINGS: EXODUS 34:4B–6, 8–9; 2 CORINTHIANS 13:11–13;
JOHN 3:16–18

[90] + WHAT A FAÇADE OF PIETY!

How many façades of piety are there, that inside are really atheism! How many ways of praying, how many religious practices are only on the surface, are only legalistic rituals! This is not the kind of worship that God wants! And we need to include ourselves in this accusation, we, the sacred ministers, that many times have made a business out of our worship such that the Lord could come into the temple with a whip and say, "My house is a house of prayer and you have made it a den of thieves."

May 21, 1978

[91] + LET THERE BE MORE AND MORE CHRISTIAN BASE COMMUNITIES

I think about this moment in this archdiocesan community, a pioneer in these four departments of the country. Its Christian Base Communities are so beautiful, so charming, where men, young people, women, get to know each other more and more deeply and feel in their hearts that what links them is the love of the Father, the grace of the Son and the communion of the Holy Spirit. Because of this, I insist so much, dear brothers and sisters, that there be more and more Christian Base Communities. It is not a discovery of this age; it is the great need that Christian people have to know one another, to love one another, to live together, having their consciousness raised in this divine energy.

May 21, 1978

[*Note:* Christian Base Communities ("Comunidades de Base") are small communities that resulted from the episcopal conference in Medellín in 1968.]

[92] + THERE ARE MANY WHO GO TO COMMUNION WHO ARE IDOLATERS

How can Christians, who are nourished in Eucharistic Communion, in which their faith says that they are united to the life of Christ, live in idolatry of money, idolatry of power, idolatry of self, selfishness? How can a Christian who receives Communion be an idolater? Well, dear brothers and sisters, there are many who go to Communion and are idolaters.

May 28, 1978

READINGS: DEUTERONOMY 8:2–3, 14B–16A; 1 CORINTHIANS
10:16–17; JOHN 6:51–59

[93] + "WHEN YOU TAKE COMMUNION, YOU RECEIVE FIRE"

If we truly believe that Christ, in the Eucharist of our Church, is the living bread that feeds the world, and that, as a believing Christian who receives this Host, I am the instrument, then I should bring it to the world. I have the responsibility of being the leavening of society, of transforming such an ugly world. This, yes, would change the face of the country, to truly inject the life of Christ in our society, in our laws, in our politics, in all our relationships. Who is going to do this? You are! If all of you, the Salvadoran Christians, don't do this, then don't expect El Salvador to be fixed. El Salvador will only be leavened with divine life if the Christians of El Salvador truly propose not to live a lazy faith, a fearful faith, rather truly as the saint—I think it was St. John Chrysostom—said, "When you take Communion, you receive fire." You ought to leave breathing joy, with the strength to transform the world.

May 28, 1978

[94] + THERE IS A HEAVINESS
IN MY POOR SPIRIT

Ah, if we had prayerful human beings among the people who control the destinies of our country, the destinies of the economy! If human beings, rather than relying on their human methods, would lean on God and on his methods, we would have a world like the one the Church dreams of: a world without injustice, a world where rights are respected, a world with the generous participation of all, a world without repression, a world without torture. And, forgive me for always mentioning torture, because there is a heaviness in my poor spirit when I think of the people who suffer lashes, kicks, blows from other people. If those who do such things had a little of God in their hearts, they would see that the person they are hurting is their brother, their brother made in the image of God. And I say this because these situations continue, people continue to be taken, to disappear. I wish, brothers and sisters, that a little contact with God from these prisons that seem to be hells, would bring down a little light and would make them understand what God wants of people. God doesn't want these things. God disapproves of evil. God wants goodness, love.

July 17, 1977

READINGS: GENESIS 18:1–10; COLOSSIANS 1:24–28;
LUKE 10:38–42

[95] + LET US NOT MEDITATE ON A WORD WITHOUT GIVING IT FLESH

Let us not meditate on a Word divorced from reality. For it is very easy to preach a Gospel that could be heard here in El Salvador, as well as in Guatemala or in Africa. It is the same Gospel, naturally, like it is the same sun that shines on all. But like the sun brings different flowers, fruits, according to the needs of the nature that receives it; also the Word of God has to take form in specific realities, and this is the difficult thing about the preaching of the Church. Preaching a Gospel with no commitment to reality doesn't cause any problems, and it is very easy in this way to carry out the mission of the preacher. But to illuminate with this universal light of the Gospel our own Salvadoran misery and also our own Salvadoran joys and successes, in this way, we know that Christ is speaking to us.

June 4, 1978

READINGS: DEUTERONOMY 18:26–28; ROMANS 3:21–25B; MATTHEW 7:21–27

[96] + JUSTICE

Today we talk a great deal about justice and perhaps we interpret it wrongly. Justice, according to the word of God for today, means action, the compassionate intervention of God, manifested in Christ, to erase sin in human beings and to give them the capacity to work as children of God.

June 4, 1978

[97] + IDOLATRY

Denouncing idolatry has always been the mission of the prophets and of the Church. Today we no longer speak of the god Baal, but there are other great idols in our time: money is a god, power, luxury, licentiousness. How many gods are enthroned in this environment! And the voice of Hosea is still contemporary today and says to Christians: Don't mix these idolatries with the worship of the true God. You can't serve two masters: the true God and money. You have to follow just one of them.

June 11, 1978

READINGS: HOSEA 6:3B–6; ROMANS 1:18–25; MATTHEW 9:9–13

[98] + GOD WALKS WITH THE HISTORY OF THE PEOPLE

God is life. God is evolution. God is newness. God walks with the history of the people. And the people, believers in God, shouldn't cling to traditions, customs; especially when these customs, these traditions cloud the true Gospel of our Lord and Savior Jesus Christ. You must be attentive to the voice of the Spirit: Be converted, follow this Gospel, this call from the Lord! Those who feel secure and think they don't need to change are Pharisees, hypocrites, whited sepulchers. They all feel very secure, but who knows about what their consciences are pricking them?

June 11, 1978

[99] + YOUR PRAYER DOESN'T PLEASE ME

Your prayer doesn't please me if it comes from a heart full of rancor. Don't pray to me, don't offer up Masses if you come with injustice, your hands stained with hate or with violence.

June 11, 1978

[100] + NO ONE FINDS IT HARDER....

No one finds it harder than I do to reveal the evil of his own people, brothers and sisters, which I have the pastoral duty to reveal—by command of the Gospel and of Jesus Christ, who takes away the sins of the world—what is sin and should not reign, what paths we should be walking. Conversion, faith and compassion are what I have always preached. Only vile and undignified slander can find anything else in my words.

June 11, 1978

[101] + TO MAKE THAT DOCTRINE BLOOD AND LIFE, TRUTH AND HISTORY

I have proved once again that I will die, God willing, faithful to the successor of Peter, the vicar of Christ. It is easy to preach his teachings in a theoretical way. To follow faithfully the magisterium of the pope in theory is very easy. But when it is about living it, making it flesh, trying to make these saving teachings reality in the history of a suffering people like ours, that is when conflicts arise. And this doesn't mean that I have become unfaithful! Never! On the contrary, I feel that today I am more faithful because I live the test, the suffering, and the intimate joy of proclaiming a doctrine that I have always believed and loved. And doing this not just with words and professions from my lips, but rather trying to give it life in the community that the Lord has entrusted to me. And, I appeal to all of you, dear brothers and sisters, that if we are truly Catholics, followers of an authentic Gospel, which, because it is authentic is very hard, if we truly want to honor this word of the heirs of Christ, let's not be afraid of making that doctrine—which from the pages of the Gospel becomes contemporary in the doctrine of the councils and of the popes, who try to live, like true shepherds, the vicissitudes of their time—blood and life, truth and history.

July 2, 1978

READINGS: 2 KINGS 4:8–11, 14–16A;

ROMANS 6:3–4, 8–11; MATTHEW 10:37–42

[102] + YOU ALL ALSO PREACH TO ME

You all, brothers and sisters, also preach to me. I know, through the theological doctrine of the Church, that this gift of infallibility, that only God possesses, he has given to the people of God. The people of God have an instrument that is the pope. The pope expresses the charism of infallibility at the same time that the people feel it and live it. You have a very fine sense that is called *sensus fidei*, sense of faith, through which a member of the people of God can detect when a preacher is not in harmony with the true doctrine revealed by God.

July 2, 1978

[103] + YOU CAN'T DO EVIL FOR A GOOD END

I repeat a great principle that is often forgotten and that has to be taken into account at all levels of morality: *Non sum facienda mala ut eveniant bona*. It is declared in Latin: You can't do evil for a good end. You can't buy freedom nor innocent dignity that has been trampled. You can't try to console the families of the disappeared by causing other families the same anguish. You can never say that the ends justify the means.

July 9, 1978

READINGS: ZECHARIAH 9:9–10; ROMANS 8:9, 11–13;
MATTHEW 11:25–30

[104] + POVERTY OF THE CHURCH

This is the true poverty of the Church, this that I have tried to preach to you, brothers and sisters. Poverty that finds its strength in its own weakness, in its own sin, but based in the compassion of Christ, in the power of the Lord. This Church doesn't want to base its strength on the support of the powerful or on politics, but rather to separate itself nobly to walk held only in the arms of the crucified one, which is its true strength.

July 9, 1978

[105] + THE BIBLE ALONE ISN'T ENOUGH

The Bible alone isn't enough. It is necessary that the Church take up the Bible again and make it living Word. Not in order to repeat exactly psalms and parables, but rather to apply it to real life at the moment in which this word of God is preached. The Bible is like a spring where this revelation, this word of God, is preserved. But, of what use is that spring, as clear as it might be, if we aren't going to put it in our pitchers and take it home to use for our needs there? A Bible that is only used to read and to live clinging in a material way to the traditions and customs of the times in which these pages were written, is a dead Bible. This is Bible worship; it is not revelation from God.

July 16, 1978

READINGS: ISAIAH 55:10–11; ROMANS 8:18–23; MATTHEW 13:1–23

[106] + YOU ALL TEACH ME

The preacher not only teaches, the preacher also learns. You all teach me. Your attention is also inspiration of the Holy Spirit for me. Your rejection would also mean for me the rejection of God.

July 16, 1978

[107] + IF YOU SPEAK, YOU HAVE TO TELL THE TRUTH

Thank God that the Church in El Salvador can still speak. But, let them not try to silence that voice, because if you speak, you have to tell the truth, and if not, better that you remain silent.

July 16, 1978

[108] + THE CHURCH IS NOT ON EARTH TO HAVE PRIVILEGES

I want us to emphasize a great deal this great teaching, because the Church is not on earth to have privileges, to lean on power or on riches, to ingratiate itself with the great ones of the world. The Church isn't here to erect great material temples or monuments either. The Church is not on earth to teach the wisdom of the earth. The Church is the kingdom of God that gives us precisely this: being children of God.

July 30, 1978

READINGS: 1 KINGS 3:5, 7–12; ROMANS 8:28–30; MATTHEW 13:33–57

[109] + CLEANSE ME, LORD

Lord, don't give me riches, don't give me a long or a short life, don't give me powers on earth that make human beings drunk with power, don't give me the madness of idolatry of the false idols of this world. Cleanse me, Lord, cleanse my intentions and give me the true wisdom of discernment, to distinguish between good and evil, give me the conviction that St. Peter had of feeling myself loved.

July 30, 1978

[110] + LET'S NOT TRY TO TAME THE GOSPEL

Let's not try to remake Christianity to suit our tastes. Let's not try to tame the Gospel, rather, let us conform ourselves to the Gospel and try to follow the authentic Christ, if we truly want to be saved.

July 30, 1978

[111] + STRUGGLE BETWEEN TRUTH AND LIES

We live in a time of struggle between truth and lies; between sincerity, which almost no one believes in still, and hypocrisy and intrigue. Let's not be afraid, brothers and sisters, let's try to be sincere, to love truth, let's try to model ourselves on Christ Jesus. It is time for us to have a great sense of selection, of discernment.

July 30, 1978

[112] + DON'T AVOID YOUR VOCATION AS LEADERS

Brothers and sisters, in the name of Christ, help to clarify reality, to look for solutions. Don't avoid your vocation as leaders. Know that what you have received from God isn't to be hidden in the comfort of a family, in well-being. Today the country needs, above all, your intelligence. The political parties, the labor organizations, cooperative or popular ones, the Lord this morning wants to inspire you with the mystique of his divine transfiguration, to also transfigure, through these organized forces, not through inefficient methods or mystiques of violence, but rather with true, authentic liberation.

August 6, 1978

READINGS: DANIEL 7:9–10, 13–14; 2 PETER 1:16–19;

MATTHEW 17:1–9

[113] + PRAYER

Humankind is the other self of God. He has elevated us to be able to speak with us and share with us his joys, his generosity, his greatness. What a divine companion in dialogue! How is it possible that we humans can live without praying! How is it possible for a human person to go through his entire life without thinking about God! Having this space for the divine empty and never filling it!

August 13, 1978

READINGS: 1 KINGS 19:9A, 11–13; ROMANS 9:1–5;

MATTHEW 14:22–23

[114] + CHRIST OVERFLOWS THE CHURCH

God is in Christ and Christ is in the Church. But the Church cannot contain Christ! That is, the Church can't say that it has a monopoly on Christ, that is to say: Only those who are in the Church are Christians. There are many who are Christians in their souls who don't know the Church, but are maybe better than those who belong to the Church. Christ overflows the Church, like when you put a glass in a well full of water, the glass fills with water but it doesn't contain the whole well, there is a great deal of water outside the glass. Thus the council says that there are many elements of truth and grace that belong to Christ that aren't in the Church. This is one of the great revelations, we could say, rediscoveries of a great truth. For those who feel vain pride in the institution of the Church, know that we can say: In the Church, not all Christians are present, nor are all present Christians. There are many Christians who are not in our Church. Blessed be God, that there are many good people, of the best, outside the confines of the Church as institution: Protestants, Jews, Muslims, etc.

August 13, 1978

[115] + CHURCH HIERARCHY

Take care, Catholics! Beginning with us, the ministers of God. Let us not think that because we are bishops and priests or because we are Church institutions, we are the best of Christianity. We are signs, but we can be like a bell that is a sign: It rings but it is left outside.

August 13, 1978

[116] + TO SERVE THE PEOPLE

I simply maintain the position that I am not confronting anyone, rather that I am trying to serve the people. Those who are in conflict with the people will be in conflict with me. But my love is the people, and from the people, you can see—by the light of faith and the mandate that God has given me to lead this people in the path of the Gospel—who is with me and who is not with me, simply by looking at their relations with the people.

August 20, 1978

READINGS: ISAIAH 56:1, 6–7; ROMANS 11:13–15, 29–32;
MATTHEW 15:21–28

[117] + THEY ASK FOR ME TO BE REMOVED

Be very careful, brothers and sisters, as Church news I tell you that I know that they are collecting signatures to send to the pope—it won't be Paul VI, it will be the new one— and to Puebla to the meeting of bishops, asking that Marxism be condemned. This is fine, but Marxism has already been condemned. This is nothing new. Pius XII already issued a document in this respect. If you aren't familiar with it, look it up. What concerns me more is this: that these signatures are also asking that I be removed. I don't have any problem with being removed, nor do I have ambitions for the power of the diocese. I only think that this is service and that as long as the Lord, through the pope, has me here, I will be faithful to my conscience according to the light of the Gospel, that is what I try to preach, no more and no less.

August 20, 1978

[118] + MY POSITION

So that you see what my position is and how I am carrying it out: I study the Word of God that is going to be read on Sunday; I look around me, at my people; I cast the light of the Word on it and I make a synthesis to be able to communicate it and make them—this people—the light of the world, so that they let themselves be guided by criteria and not by the idolatries of earth. Because of that, naturally, the idols of the earth are bothered by this Word and they would like to uproot it, to silence it, to kill it. May God's will be done, but his Word, St. Paul said, cannot be chained up. There will be prophets, priests, or laypeople—there are already many of them—who understand what God wants through his word and for our people.

August 20, 1978

READINGS: ISAIAH 56:1, 6–7; ROMANS 11:13–15, 29–32;

MATTHEW 15:21–28

[119] + THE RIGHT TO ORGANIZE

No one can deprive people of the right to join together as long as they are joining together to support a just cause. We are not defending criminal groups, whatever sector they may be in. If it is to kidnap, rob, or kill, there is no right to do this. But uniting in order to survive, to eat, to defend one's rights—every person has a right to do this. Joining together is a right when the objectives are just. And the Church will always be on the side of this right to organize and the just objectives of these organizations.

August 20, 1978

[120] + THE SPIRITUAL MEANING OF LIFE

This is the mission of the Church: to awaken, like I am doing at this moment, the spiritual meaning of life, the divine worth of human action. Don't lose this, dear brothers and sisters. This is what the Church offers to organizations, to politics, to industry, to commerce, to the day laborer, to the woman in the market, the Church brings this service of promoting spiritual dynamism to everyone.

August 20, 1978

[121] + I AM NOT AN EXPERT

I am not an expert in sociology, nor in politics, nor in organization, only a simple pastor who is saying to those who are experts: Join together, put yourselves, everything you know, at the service of the people. Don't shut yourselves in, contribute. Only then will there be rights and justice.

August 20, 1978

[122] + THE DISAPPEARED

It is not politics, brothers and sisters, what I am about to say. In our archdiocese, we have carried out a very detailed study of the disappeared. We have carefully analyzed ninety-nine cases. We have the name, age, where they were taken, what legal efforts were made on their behalf, how many times the mother has gone to look for her dear one. I am a witness to the truth of these ninety-nine cases. Because of this, I have every right to ask: Where are they? And to say, in the name of the anguish of this people: Bring them before a court if they are alive, and if, unfortunately, the agents of the security forces have already killed them, hold them responsible and invoke sanctions on them, whomever they might be. The one who has killed must pay. I think this demand is just.

August 20, 1978

[123] + THE LAW IS LIKE A SNAKE

The other study that we have done is an analysis of the Law of Defense and the Guarantee of Public Order.... In it, we studied specific recent cases of the application of this law that is doing real damage, especially to our poor. Because a poor person said something to me that you will never forget, just as I won't: "The law, Archbishop, is like a snake: it only stings those of us who go barefoot." In the study, we also collected the statements of repudiation, they are voices of the people that we must listen to.

August 20, 1978

[124] + THE MARTYRS

Yesterday, Saturday the twenty-sixth, in Tejutla, when we celebrated the first anniversary of the death of Felipe de Jesús Chacón, I also realized that our land offers to the pope, like I told him in my previous visits, martyrs! I was horrified when they told me! Felipe de Jesús's face with no skin on it and what is even worse, slandered in the press as a cattle thief, when he was really a brave catechist who followed the Gospel to its most dangerous consequences.

August 27, 1978

READINGS: ISAIAH 22:19–23; ROMANS 11:33–36;

MATTHEW 16:13–20

[125] + HEARTS OVERFLOWING WITH THE GOSPEL

The Church doesn't have a wish, an intention of speaking only in order to denounce. I am the one who feels, more than anyone else, repugnance at saying such things! But I feel that it is my duty, that it is not being grandiose, but is merely the truth. And we have to see the truth with our eyes wide open and our feet firmly planted on the ground, but with our hearts full to bursting with the Gospel and of God, in order to search for solutions, not to violent, cruel, and criminal things which have just happened, but rather the solution of justice. Only justice can be the root of peace.

August 27, 1978

[126] + THE WILL OF GOD

Let us not attribute to God the fruits of our laziness. Let us not blame God for unjust inequalities. Let us not blame God for the underdevelopment of humankind. God does not want these things.

September 3, 1978
READINGS: JEREMIAH 20:7–9; ROMANS 12 :1–2;
MATTHEW 16:21–27

[127] + FALSE PRUDENCE

The cross provokes Christ himself to defend his mission, which is cross and sacrifice. How easy it is to act like St. Peter, flee like today many Christians are fleeing. It is easier to hide. "Let's not create conflict. Prudence! We have to be more prudent." But Christ didn't think this way and he called the one who advised him not to put himself in danger Satan, he called him scandal.

September 3, 1978

[128] + PRESSURES

How awful are pressures when they try to separate us from what God wants, so that we do what humans want!

September 3, 1978

[129] + TOUCHSTONE

You all know how silversmiths establish the authenticity ⌐. ⌐⌐.⌐.
or gold. There is a touchstone, they touch it to the stone to
see if it produces sound and calculate the carats. The cross is
our touchstone. We hit our life on the cross and we see what it
sounds like. It sounds like cowardice, like fear, like the thoughts
of humans and not of God. The cross is the authentic proof of
the person who wants to follow Christ. Because of this the Lord
says: Let those who want to follow me take up their crosses.

September 3, 1978

[130] + GOD AND SUFFERING

Christianity isn't a kind of masochism, that philosophy of
suffering for suffering's sake, or that stoicism of the Greeks of
suffering for the sake of suffering. No! God didn't make us to
suffer. God made us for happiness.

September 3, 1978

[131] + WITHOUT THE CROSS LIFE IS A FAILURE

Without the cross life is a failure. What does it mean to not embrace the cross? What is the failure in our lives? St. Paul, in today's second reading, tells us not to be conformed to this world. That is to throw aside the cross: to be conformed to this world and not to follow the cross. The world says that money is happiness and Christ says blessed are the poor in spirit! Christ says that we have to forgive and the world repeats the pagan *adagio*: an eye for an eye, a tooth for a tooth, revenge, violence, and hatred. Don't conform yourselves, then, to the world's thought. And so we can continue to describe in infinity two lines that grow ever farther apart: the line of conformity with the will of God and the line of conformity with this world.

September 3, 1978

[132] + IT IS SAD TO HAVE TO LEAVE ONE'S COUNTRY

It's sad to have to leave one's country because, in that country, there is not a just order where one can find work.

September 3, 1978

[133] + I AM NOT A BOSS

The authority of the Church is not in giving orders, it is in service. I ask forgiveness, from my community, when I have not been able to function as your servant in my role as bishop. I am not a boss; I am not someone who merely gives orders; I am not an authority that is imposed. I want to be the servant of God and of all of you.

September 10, 1978

READINGS: EZEKIEL 33:7–9; ROMANS 13:8–10; MATTHEW 18:15–20

[134] + PERSONAL AND SOCIAL SIN

Many are scandalized, they say that sin is personal and not societal. Certainly the Bible of today tells us: The evildoer will be lost
because of his guilt. But it has also mentioned the shared responsibility of the prophet who does not prophesy. Those who allow
injustice to exist, especially if they could avoid it, every family
that prostitutes itself with selfishness and doesn't have a Christian
sense of life, every home that is not sanctified as God wants it to
be sanctified and in which they are living in sin, is contaminated.
They have become accomplices. They have committed social
sin. And the atmosphere—like that in El Salvador—becomes
such that they even decree a law to preserve order. What order?
It is the order of injustice that is not to be questioned. The situation is to be maintained, not denounced, because that would be
sticking your nose in politics. El Salvador is in a state of institutionalized sin.

September 10, 1978

[135] + I LOVE YOU VERY MUCH

Dear brothers and sisters, especially you my dear brothers and
sisters that hate me, you my dear brothers and sisters that think
that I am preaching violence, and defame me and know it is not
true, you who have hands stained with crime, with torture, with
abuse, with injustice: be converted! I love you very much, but
you cause me sorrow, because you are on the road to hell.

September 10, 1978

[136] + CHRISTIAN BASE COMMUNITIES

How could my heart not be filled with hope by a Church where the Christian Base Communities flourish! And why should I not ask my dear brother priests to make these communities flourish everywhere, in the *barrios*, in the tiny villages, in families!

September 10, 1978

[137] + THE WILL OF GOD

It is not the will of God for some to have everything and for others to have nothing. This cannot be of God. It is his will that all his children be happy.

September 10, 1978

[138] + THE CHURCH EXISTS TO SERVE

A church cannot only be concerned with taking care of itself, like those who live obsessed only with their health and never have time to do anything else, because they are taking care of their health. The Church takes care of its health, but not through selfishness, rather so that it might be strong and healthy, and serve. The Church has as its goal to serve.

September 17, 1978

[139] + PLURALISM IN THE CHURCH

You, with your charismatic movement: you, with your *Cursillo* movement of Christianity; you, with your community studying catechism; you, with your traditional thoughts; you, with your progressive thoughts, why do you do this? Do you defend what you do because it is comfortable? Then you are going the wrong way. This is not the right thing to do. Do you do it in order to serve God sincerely? Well, do it this way and try to understand others who do what they are doing for God. This is true pluralism in the Church.

September 17, 1978

[140] + THE NATIONAL ANTHEM

The national anthem is not dogma and contains a great deal that is beautiful and true. We have to bring this beauty and truth to the reality of the country, so that we are not singing about something that doesn't really exist, and so that we make the beauty of the anthem reality in this country.

September 24, 1978

READINGS: ISAIAH 55:6–9; PHILIPPIANS 1:20C–24, 27A;
MATTHEW 20:1–16

[141] + SERVICE TO HUMANKIND

We shouldn't see professions only as a way to earn money and establish ourselves politically or socially. We have to seek, as the young people are doing now, service to humankind, the best use of my life, not to earn but rather to serve.

September 24, 1978

[142] + GOD IN MY POCKET

Many actually want, like the song says, a pocket God, a God that accommodates to their idols, a God that is content with what I pay my day laborers, a God that approves my abuses of others. How can some people pray to this God the Our Father if they treat him as one of their servants or workers?

September 24, 1978

[143] + GOD CALLS YOU AND FORGIVES YOU

I repeat again what I have said so many times on the radio speaking to those who perhaps are the cause of so much injustice and violence, those who have caused weeping in so many homes, those who are stained with blood from so many murders, those whose hands are stained by torture, those who have silenced their consciences, that aren't moved when they see a man humiliated under their heel, suffering, perhaps about to die. To all of them, I say: Your crimes don't matter, they are ugly, horrible, you have violated the most dignified part of a human being, but God calls you and forgives you.

September 24, 1978

[144] + KENOSIS

Kenosis means to empty oneself, throw off the rank of God, as if a sovereign were to leave his throne and mantle and everything, and dress in peasant rags to go among the peasants without disrupting them with his presence as a king. Christ dresses himself in humanity and appears as an ordinary man. If Christ were present here, in the cathedral, among the people that have the goodness to be listening to me, I would not recognize him. And knowing that he was the son of God in the form of a man! And, even more than that, it wasn't enough for him to look like a man, but he also humiliated himself to take on the form of a slave to die like a slave, crucified on a cross, like a thief, like a castoff of Israel who was to be crucified outside the city, like trash. This is Christ, the God that humiliated himself through this kenosis, through this profound emptying of who he was.

October 1, 1978
READINGS: EZEKIEL 18:25–28; PHILIPPIANS 2:1–11;
MATTHEW 21:28–32

[145] + HUMBLE AND POOR CHURCH

Dear brothers and sisters, this is the glory of the Church; to carry inside itself all the kenosis of Christ. And because of this, it has to be humble and poor. A lofty Church, a Church that depends on earthly powers, a Church without kenosis, a Church full of pride, a self-sufficient Church, this is not the Church of St. Paul's kenosis.

October 1, 1978

[146] + NON-CHRISTIANS

Brothers and sisters, what goodness, what truth, how much good there is beyond the Christian borders! We must respect this. Because many times we think that because we are in the Church that we are the world's best. Who knows whether here, in the Church, we are less good, less noble, less human than those outside.

October 8, 1978

READINGS: ISAIAH 5:1–7; PHILIPPIANS 4:6–9; MATTHEW 21:33–43

[147] + FANATICISM

Let us not be fanatics! Fanaticism among Christians has done a great deal of harm.

October 8, 1978

[148] + THE GOD THAT WEEPS

How different our country would be if we were reaping what God has sown! But God feels he has failed with certain societies. And I think that the pages of Isaiah and of St. Paul on this Sunday show the sad Salvadoran reality: I expected rule of law and you have murders; I expected justice and you have laments. It does not mean that we sow discord here, it is simply to cry out to the God that weeps; to the God that feels the laments of his people, because there is much abuse; the God that feels the laments of his peasants who can't sleep in their homes because they have to flee during the night, the lament of children that cry out for their mama and papa who have disappeared: Where are they? This is not what God hoped for. The Salvadoran homeland like the one we are living in is not what should be the fruit of a seed of humanism and Christianity.

October 8, 1978

[149] + JUSTICE IS OUR STRENGTH

If they control all the media, why are they worried about a radio transmitter and a small newspaper? Justice is our strength; the truth is what makes the smallness of out media great. That is why they fear it.

October 8, 1978

[150] + THEY AREN'T GOING TO GET ME TO CHANGE MY PREACHING

How beautiful the attitude of the independent man, the man that doesn't alter his preaching and his Church to get financial support. This is costing our Church a great deal, brothers and sisters. This autonomy from the idol of money, from the idol of power and presenting ourselves to the world like Paul, audaciously free. Appreciating those who give to us, but knowing that they aren't necessary, that because of doing this they aren't going to get me to change my preaching. Thank you very much, but know that I owe my allegiance to God and not to you. Thank you very much, but know that even though you might have forgotten me, I would love you anyway and I would preach the same way.

October 15, 1978

READINGS: ISAIAH 25:6–10A; PHILIPPIANS 4:12–14, 19–20;
MATTHEW 22:1–14

[151] + THE CHURCH OF THE POOR

Here Christ is giving us the answer to a slander that we hear frequently: Why does the Church only preach to the poor? Why the Church of the poor? Don't we rich have souls too? Of course and we love you deeply and we want you to be saved. We don't want you to perish imprisoned in your own idolatry. We ask you to become spiritual, to become poor souls, feel the necessity, the anguish of those in need.

October 15, 1978

[152] + IT'S NOT ENOUGH TO ATTEND MASS

It's not enough to attend Mass on Sunday; it is not enough to call yourself a Catholic. It is not enough to bring your child to be baptized, even though this be at a big society party. Appearances are not enough. God is not satisfied with appearance. God wants the garment of justice. God wants his Christians dressed in love.

October 15, 1978

[153] + THE CHURCH OF THE POOR

The well-being of the Church can lead to laxness. Priests who feel very content in their parishes, be careful! Christians who are not bothered by the Gospel, be careful! It was to this comfortable worship that Malachi referred in his terrible prophecy, "Now it touches you, priests. You have deviated from the path, you have made many stumble on the law. I will make you despised, vile before the people" [Malachi 2:8–9]. There is nothing worse than a bad priest. If the salt loses its flavor, what good is it? There is nothing to do—said Christ—but to throw it on the floor and let people step on it. How sad are the words of a priest when he has lost credibility: a rattling can! "You haven't kept to my paths. You look at who people are when you apply the law" [Matthew 5:13]. If it is Mr. X, if it is Mrs. Y, with great pleasure. If it is a poor, despised person, you pay no attention to him. The Church of the poor is a seal of authenticity, because it is not a class-based Church. I don't mean that I despise the rich, rather I mean to say to them that if they do not become poor of heart they will not be able to enter the kingdom of heaven. The one who truly preaches Christ is the Church of the poor, to be found in poverty, in misery, in the hope of the one who prays amid turbulence, in pain, in not being heard. There is a God that hears, and only by coming closer to this voice can one also feel God. "You look at who people are when you apply the law." How well the peasant expressed it: law is like a snake, it only stings those who go barefoot!

November 5, 1978

READINGS: MALACHI 1:14B—2:2B, 8–10;
THESSALONIANS 2:7–9, 13; MATTHEW 23:1–12

[154] + CHRISTIAN

St. Teresa already said it, we are already confused as to what title we have to give to prelates: whether to call them "your excellence," or "your eminence." By now we don't understand this, many times it seems ludicrous: Your excellence, your excellence! How much more beautiful is the simple name of Christian!

November 5, 1978

[155] + FAITH AND DAILY LIFE

How many have come to what the council says, "the separation between faith and the daily lives of many must be considered as one of the gravest errors of this time." Those who make religion consist solely of a few acts of worship, but who after this worship—a *Te Deum* for a fifteenth birthday [a social custom for Hispanic girls], weddings in which matrimony is not seen as the love of Christ for the Church but rather a simple social relationship, looking to see if it was better than another wedding at which there were so many thousands of expenses—all this worship seems at times to satisfy human vanity. But then the person lives, besides their participation in these acts of worship, with injustice, violating the right of assembly of his workers that want to form a union, not paying well those who cut his coffee. Ah, they say, he is very religious because he goes to Mass every Sunday! These acts of worship are meaningless when they are separated from your daily life. The Church has to preach to men and women that in temporal things they have to remember that they will have to account to God.

November 12, 1978
READINGS: WISDOM 6:13–17; THESSALONIANS 4:12–17;
MATTHEW 25:1–13

[156] + AN INDIVIDUALISTIC WAY OF THINKING

One of the most pressing messages of the Church today is that Christians leave behind their individualistic ways of thinking. That we no longer talk about "my" salvation, "my" religion, rather we live it like God wants us to live it: as a people. It is our salvation, our path through history. We go as a people, like the Israelites through the desert: They went together, as a community, that's the way we should go. And, because of this, one of the greatest joys as a pastor is to see communities springing up everywhere.

November 19, 1978

READINGS: PROVERBS 31:10–13, 19–20, 30–31; 1 THESSALONIANS 5:1–6; MATTHEW 25:14–30

[157] + PIETY OF SONGS AND PRAYERS

It is very pretty to like a piety only of songs and prayers, only of spiritual meditation, only of contemplation. The hour for such things will come in heaven, where there won't be any injustices, where sin will not be a reality that Christians will have to dethrone. Now, Christ said to the contemplative apostles on Mount Tabor who wanted to stay there forever, let's go down, we have work to do.

November 19, 1978

[158] + THE CHURCH IS NOT A REARVIEW MIRROR

I say that it is a satisfaction for me to see that I am in harmony with what I modestly wanted to be, also for the benefit of my dear archdiocese. I also feel linked to my predecessors: to Bishop Chavez, to Bishop Belloso, to Bishop Pérez y Aguilar; and I don't need anyone to come comparing who might be better than I am. What I need are those who will help me to live this present moment. The Church is not memories, it is not merely a rearview mirror. The Church continues to move forward and also needs new perspectives. Let us give thanks that a whole tradition has brought us to this moment in which the people have faith. Blessed be those who came before us! But let us know how to be men and women of the now and let us reflect on what has happened this week, in this moment. There are many who do not want us to put our fingers on the sore spot, to look at the present; and, in this way, they want to live as if in a museum, on memories, on comparisons with earlier bishops. The pope speaks of the moment and I want to speak each week of the moment that we are living.

November 26, 1978

READINGS: EZEKIEL 34:11–12, 15–17;
1 CORINTHIANS 15:20–26, 28; MATTHEW 25:31–46

[159] + THE GREATEST THING IN THE CHURCH IS YOU

The greatest thing in the Church is you, you who are not priests nor nuns, but rather who are in the heart of the world, are married, in your professions, in business, in the market. In the work of each day, you are those who are making the world run and you are the ones who have to sanctify it according to God's wishes.

November 26, 1978

[160] + YOUR FRIEND

A little girl said to me upon arriving, "Let us children and the young people greet you as a good friend." No one has ever said anything more beautiful to me: I want to be your friend.

November 26, 1978

[161] + APPLAUSE

What do I want more than your applause! It is not because applause is a profanation of the temple, rather it is a free and spontaneous expression of a people that feels what cannot be said in words and says it in this nice way. I, then, want to thank you because all of this means that the pastoral and evangelical path that I try to be faithful to is not craziness nor subversion, rather it is simply humble faithfulness to the commandment of the Lord.

November 26, 1978

[162] + THE FINAL JUDGMENT

I don't want to be on the left in the hour of the final judgment, "Go away from here, evildoer, to the eternal fire, because I was hungry and you didn't give me anything to eat, I was in need and you didn't help me" [Matthew 25:35].You were too concerned about the purity of your orthodoxy, about your quiet time for prayer, about your congregation, your school, to soil yourself with the miserable ones. You were more concerned about your social, political and economic prestige, and, for this reason, you looked down on me when I was the one asking you for help.

November 26, 1978

[163] + THE FACE OF CHRIST

The face of Christ amid the bags and baskets of those who pick coffee. The face of Christ amid tortures and mistreatment in the jails. The face of Christ dying of hunger amid the children who have nothing to eat. The face of Christ in the needy people who ask the Church to speak for them.

November 26, 1978

[164] + THE PRESENCE OF CHRIST

It would be shame to have lived so surrounded with the presence of Christ, because we are surrounded with the poor, and not to have recognized him. To have lived so many years in comfort, with riches, politically well off and not to have been concerned with that Christ who was at our doors or whom we met in the streets.

November 26, 1978

[165] + THE CHURCH OF THE POOR

When we speak of the Church of the poor we are not using Marxist dialectic, as if the Church of the rich were another. What we are saying is that Christ, inspired by the Spirit of God, said, "The Lord has sent me to bring the Gospel to the poor" [Luke 4:18]—words from the Bible—to say that to hear him, it is necessary to become poor.

December 3, 1978

READINGS: ISAIAH 63:16B–17, 64:1, 3B–8; 1 CORINTHIANS 1:3–9;

MARK 13:33–37

[166] + THE CHURCH AND THE KINGDOM OF GOD

Outside the Church, anyone who struggles for justice, anyone who makes just demands in an unjust atmosphere, is working for the kingdom of God. This person may not be a Christian. The Church doesn't have a monopoly on the kingdom of God. The kingdom of God goes beyond the borders of the Church, and, for this reason, the Church values all those in agreement with its struggle to implant the kingdom of God. A Church that tries merely to keep itself pure, uncontaminated, this would not be a church at the service of humankind.

December 3, 1978

[167] + THE WORD REMAINS

The Word remains and this is great comfort for the one who preaches. My voice may disappear, but my Word, which is Christ, will remain in the hearts of those who want to keep it.

December 17, 1978

READINGS: ISAIAH 61:1–2, 10–11; 1 THESSALONIANS 5:16–24;

JOHN 1:6–8, 19–28

[168] + I AM A FRAGILE MAN

I feel that there is something new in the archdiocese. I am a fragile, limited man. I don't know what it is that is happening, but I do know that God knows. And my role as pastor is what St. Paul says today, "Don't extinguish the Holy Spirit!" [1 Thessalonians 5:19]. If, in an authoritarian way, I were to tell a priest "Don't do this!" or a Christian community, "Don't go there!", if I were to set myself up as if I were the Holy Spirit and I were going to make a church the way I want it to be, I would be extinguishing the Holy Spirit.

December 17, 1978

[169] + MARY

Mary is the expression of the need the Salvadorans have. Mary is the expression of the anguish of those who are in jail. Mary is the sorrow of the mothers who have lost their children and no one will tell them where they are. Mary is the tenderness that searches in anguish for a solution. In our country, Mary is like a street that is a dead end, but is hoping that God will come to save us. I wish that we would imitate this poor one of Jehovah and feel that without God we can't do anything, that God is the hope of our people, that only Christ, the Divine Savior, can be the savior [salvador] of our country.

December 24, 1978

READINGS: 2 SAMUEL 7:1–5, 8B–11, 16;

ROMANS 16:25–27; LUKE 1:26–38

[170] + MARY BECOMES SALVADORAN

Mary becomes Salvadoran and makes Christ flesh in the history of El Salvador. And Mary takes on your last name and my last name to bring forth the history of your family, of my family, in the eternal life of the Gospel. Mary identifies with each one of us to make Christ live in our individual story. We are blessed if we really make devotion to the Virgin consist of this. Because of this, the council warned preachers to be very careful not to promote a false idea of devotion to the Virgin that, unfortunately, has separated us from the Protestants, because some Catholics have made their devotion to the Virgin idolatry, Mary-worship. But the true doctrine is that Mary is not an idol. The only savior is God as Christ Jesus. Mary is the human instrument, the daughter of Adam, the daughter of Israel, incarnation of a people, sister of our race, who, because of her sanctity, was able to incarnate in history the divine life of God. So then, the true homage that a Christian can pay to the Virgin is to make, like she did, the effort to incarnate the life of God in the vicissitudes of our transitory history.

December 24, 1978

[171] + THE CHURCH OF THE POOR

The Church preaches from the poor and we are never ashamed to say: the Church of the poor, because, it was among the poor that Christ wanted to give his message of redemption.

December 24, 1978

READINGS: ISAIAH 9:2–7; TITUS 2:11–14; LUKE 2:1–14

[172] + TO BE HUMAN

Before being Christians, we first have to be very human. Perhaps because many times people want to build Christianity on false human bases, we have false people and false Christians, the *beato* [falsely devout] is a false Christian, and isn't fully human either. Many who now defend—they say—religion, are not even fully human and much less Christian. I laugh at these biased defenses of Christianity, by "authentic Catholics." What right do they have to call themselves authentic Catholics, if they aren't even fully human beings who know how to worship the true God, and they are idolaters, down on their knees before the things of the earth?

December 31, 1978

[173] + STUMBLING BLOCK

Christ is a stumbling block! Because of this they do me a great honor when they reject me, because, in this, I resemble in a small way Jesus Christ who also was a stumbling block.

December 31, 1978

[174] + THE CHURCH AND THE POPULAR ORGANIZATIONS

Don't think it strange that the Church supports what is just, what is good, even if this is in organizations that are called "clandestine," [usually guerilla organizations], because if what they seek is just, it is the kingdom of God.

January 7, 1979

READINGS: ISAIAH 60:1–6; EPHESIANS 3:2–3A, 5–6;

MATTHEW 2:1–12

[175] + FAITH

Faith doesn't only mean believing with the head but also committing your heart and your life.

January 7, 1979

[176] + HE CAME FROM A SMALL VILLAGE

Jesus of Nazareth, as the son of that carpenter's shop, was no
more than a human like any of the rest of us. How many times
am I overcome by the reality that if Christ lived today, in 1979,
and were thirty or thirty-three years old, he would be indistin-
guishable from the rest of you men. A man thirty-three years old
wouldn't stick out. Perhaps he would come from a small village;
he would come with his mother, the Virgin. No one would recognize him, perhaps he would be here among us, too!

January 14, 1979

READINGS: ISAIAH 42:1–4, 6–7; ACTS 10:34–38; MARK 1:6B–11

[177] + MORE IMPORTANT THAN MY PERSONAL SAFETY

Thank you very much, Mr. President, for listening to me. I also
want to thank you for having offered me protection were I to ask
for it. I appreciate it, but I want to reiterate my position on this:
that I never seek my own personal advantage, rather I seek the
good of my priests and of my people.... More important than
my personal safety, I would wish for safety and tranquility for
108 families and disappeared people, for all those who suffer.
Personal well-being, protection for my life isn't something that I
want as long as I see my people subject to an economic, political,
and social system that constantly tends to widen these social
differences.

January 14, 1979

[178] + THE CHURCH AND THE GOVERNMENT

Realize that the conflict isn't between the Church and the government. It is between the government and the people. The Church is with the people and the people are with the Church, thank God!

January 21, 1979
READINGS: JONAH 3:1–5, 10; 1 CORINTHIANS 7:29–31;
MARK 1:14–20

[179] + IMPUNITY

Let there not be so many crimes and abuses with impunity and, even though they may wear military uniforms, they must face justice and give an accounting for what they have done and to receive appropriate punishment if it has to do with common crimes.

February 18, 1979
READINGS: ISAIAH 43:18–19, 21–22, 24B–25;
2 CORINTHIANS 1:18–22; MARK 2:1–13

[180] + THE BAALS OF OUR DAYS

The Baals were the gods of fertility. The harvests were attributed to them, the rains, the sun. And the prophet (Hosea) cried out throughout his book: It is not the baals, it is not the idols that give Israel bread, it is the true God. Be converted away from your idolatry! The voice of the prophet seems current when new baals in our day want to be adored instead of the only one who loves us and demands our love. Idols, baals of our day, are: idolatry of power, of wealth, of luxury, of sex.

February 25, 1979
READINGS: HOSEA 2:14B, 19–20;
2 CORINTHIANS 3:1B–6; MARK 2:18–22

[181] + CHANGE IN STRUCTURES

Everything in life is evolution. The Church renews itself. We can't cling to old traditions that no longer have a reason to exist. Even less structures in which sin has been enthroned and, as a result of these structures there are attacks, injustice, disorder. We cannot call a society, a government, or a situation Christian, when these out-of-date and unjust structures make our brothers and sisters suffer so.

February 25, 1979

[182] + SUNDAY MASS

Coming to Mass on Sunday is to come to make our alliance with God real. Each Sunday Mass is living the alliance that makes me respect God and feel God to be the only true God. Facing him, I have to dethrone all the idols that want to take God's place in my heart or in my people: the idols of power, of wealth, licentiousness, the idols of all of these things that separate men from God. Sunday has to be for us the alliance with the Lord that is renewed.

March 4, 1979

READINGS: GENESIS 9:8–15; 1 PETER 3:18–22; MARK 1:12–15

[183] + CONSUMER SOCIETY

"Giving up something frees the self from slavery to a civilization that encourages us more and more to comfort and to consumerism without any concern for protecting our environment, the common patrimony of humanity." Pay attention to these words which even serve for worldly matters! We are victims of a consumer society, of luxury. And we are buying consumer goods, because the advertising is overwhelming, and we buy things which are beyond our means. We want to live in luxury, we want to consume like everyone else does and we are becoming victims, slaves.

March 4, 1979

[Note: Romero is quoting from Pope John Paul I's 1979 Lenten message (*L'osservatore Romano*, no, 9, March 4, 1979, 12).]

[184] + THE CHURCH OF THE POOR

When we speak of the Church of the poor we are simply saying to the rich as well: Turn your gaze to this Church and concern yourselves with the poor as your own problem.

March 4, 1979

[185] + PERSECUTION

Persecution is an element that characterizes the authentic Church. If a Church doesn't suffer persecution, but rather is enjoying the privileges and support of earthly things, beware! This is not the true Church of Jesus Christ. This does not mean that this life of martyrdom and suffering, of fear and persecution is normal, but rather that it should imply a spirit of Christianity. It's not just being with the Church when things are going well, but also to follow Jesus Christ with the enthusiasm of that apostle who said, "if it is necessary, we will die with him" [Matthew 26:35].

March 11, 1979

READINGS: GENESIS 22:1–2, 9A, 15–18; ROMANS 8:31B–34;
MARK 9:1–9

[186] + CONFLICTS

If our archdiocese has become a conflictive diocese, without a doubt, it is because of its desire to be faithful to this new evangelization. From Vatican II until now and in the Latin American Bishops' meetings, they are requiring that it be a very committed kind of evangelization, fearless. A demanding evangelization that points out dangers and gives up privileges, and that does not fear conflict when this conflict arises merely as a result of faithfulness to the Lord.

March 11, 1979

READINGS: ACTS 4:32–35; 1 JOHN 5:1–6; JOHN 20:19–31

[187] + THE ENVIRONMENT

You all know that the air, the water, everything that we touch, everything in our lives is polluted. And in spite of this nature that we are polluting more and more and that we need, we don't realize that we made a commitment to God that this nature is to be cared for by humankind. Cutting down a tree, throwing out water when water is scarce, not being concerned with the exhaust of the buses, poisoning our atmosphere with foul-smelling smoke, not being careful where we burn trash—all of this is covered by our covenant with God. Let's take care of it, dear Salvadoran brothers and sisters, also out of a religious spirit, that we not keep on impoverishing and killing nature.

March 11, 1979

[188] + CORRUPTION

We could cite truly shameful situations of people who should be giving us an example of honesty in their government posts, in their businesses, with their wealth. And why do they take advantage of these posts, these situations? Nothing is done now for the common good; it is done out of selfishness. Ah, yes, there is reckoning to be made! We ask for accountability in public works! The law of God has not been respected by the very ones who should be models—the legislators, those who command. Naturally, the example of these higher-ups create doubt and uncertainty in the people and also a desire to take advantage. Then, we have a corrupt nation from top to bottom, because all of them have forgotten the law of God. We have forgotten the law of God.

March 18, 1979

READINGS: EXODUS 20:1–17; CORINTHIANS 1:22–25;
JOHN 2:13–25

[189] + THOU SHALT NOT STEAL

Thou shalt not steal! What examination of conscience can we make here, brothers and sisters, when stealing seems to be becoming the thing to do. The person who doesn't steal is considered stupid. And the one who makes a deal or starts a project and doesn't get his bribe—sometimes in the millions—hasn't known how to take advantage of the situation. Thou shalt not steal! The country would be different if there weren't so much stealing. I want to be fair with many people who have money and who are very honest, and they complain that they are blamed for everything. They make us look in another direction and say that it is not just the fourteen families that are to blame. The last names are multiplying: Former employees are leaving the government well-provided for the future. Their properties, homes, businesses are multiplying. Did you come by all of this honestly? If so, God's blessing! But, if, really, it is against the seventh commandment, the Lord will not bless it. Thou shalt not steal! It is the truth: You have stolen what you have. You have stolen it from the people that are dying in misery. You have stolen it. Brothers and sisters, stealing is always sin.

March 18, 1979

[190] + NONBELIEVERS

It is God that makes use of people, even if they are pagans, even if they don't have Christian faith. These people are instruments of God to save, to love, to give encouragement, to give hope.

March 25, 1979

READINGS: 2 CHRONICLES 36:14–16, 19–23;
EPHESIANS 2:4–10; JOHN 3:14–21

[191] + INTERIORITY

This is the message of interiority with which the Word of God today invites us to live a religion that is not one of the ten commandments and dogmas, a group of theories, rather of personal, intimate choices, beyond external practices and places and things. Let's not make religion consist of external things, but rather of sincerity, of an intimate search for God, which will produce the fruits of love, justice, sincerity, and truth. And we are living this every day, brothers and sisters. When we are friends with a person, we are not looking for payment in externals, we don't notice outward signs as much. Above all, we appreciate their sincerity, esteem, love. God's relation with humankind is like this, a relation in which it is true that there is a hierarchy, some external structure, but this isn't what is most important. All the beauty of our Church buildings wouldn't matter, all the magnificence of our rituals, if we didn't have a heart that speaks with love, with friendship, to the Lord.

April 1, 1979

READINGS: JEREMIAH 32:31–34; HEBREWS 5:7–9;
JOHN 12:20–33

[192] + GIVING OUR LIVES FOR OTHERS

Christ is saying to each one of us: If you want your life and your mission to be fruitful like mine, do as I have: Be converted into grain that is buried. Let yourself be killed; don't be afraid. The one who avoids suffering will end up alone. There is no one more alone than selfish people. But if, out of love for others, you give your life for others, like I am going to give mine, you will have an abundant harvest; you will experience the deepest satisfaction. Don't be afraid of death or of threats. The Lord is with you. He who wants to save his soul, as the Bible says, the one who wants to be well off, who doesn't want to make commitments, who doesn't want to get involved in problems, the one who wants to stay on the sidelines in a situation in which we all have to commit ourselves—this one will lose his life. How awful it would be to have lived in comfort, without any suffering, staying out of problems, very tranquil, well placed, well-connected politically, economically, and socially. Not needing anything, having it all. What good will it do? They will lose their souls. But those who, because of love of me, leave their positions and accompany the poor, and enter into the suffering of the people, incarnate, and feel the pain, the attacks, as their own, these will earn their lives, because my Father will reward them.

April 1, 1979

[193] + CIVILIZATION OF LOVE

A civilization of love is not sentimentality; it is justice and truth. A civilization of love that did not demand justice for people, would not be true civilization, it would not define authentic relations between people. Because of this, it is only a caricature of love when we want to patch with charity what is owed in justice; cover with the appearance of benevolence that we are failing in social justice. True love consists in demanding of the relationships with those we love what is just.

April 12, 1979
READINGS: ACTS 4:32–35; 1 JOHN 5:1–6; JOHN 20:19–31

[194] + LOVE AND TRUTH

Many times people say pretty words, they shake hands, and, maybe even they exchange kisses, but there is really no sincerity in this. Because of this, a civilization in which one person has lost confidence in the others, in which there is so much lying, in which there is no truth, there is no base of love. There can't be love where there are lies. The truth is lacking in our environment.

April 12, 1979

[195] + PROPHETIC PREACHING

To have the ability to see the truth is to suffer the interior torment of the prophets. Because it is much easier to preach lies, to conform to the situation so as to not lose your advantages, so that you always have friends that flatter you, so that you have power. What an awful temptation the Church has! And, nevertheless, she, who has received the spirit of truth, has to be careful not to betray the truth, and, if necessary, to lose all her privileges. She will lose them, but she will always speak the truth.

April 22, 1979

[196] + PREACHING AND CONFLICTS

Preaching virtue faced with vice creates conflicts with vice. Preaching justice when faced with injustice provokes conflicts with injustice. The Gospel the Church preaches will always provoke conflicts. Always when the Church wants to be coherent with its founder, with the breath of the Spirit that gave him the message to bring to the world, it will either betray its fidelity to that Spirit or it will lose the advantages of the sinful world. And it is preferable to stay with the Christ that dies, but later is resurrected, than to have the advantages of those who persecuted Christ, who in order to save their life in this world, will lose it.

April 22, 1979

[197] + WE HAVE NO RIGHT TO BE SAD

We have no right to be sad. A Christian can't be a pessimist. Christians must always keep the fullness of joy alive in their heart. Try this experiment, brothers and sisters—I have tried to do it many times and in the bitterest hours of situations when lies and persecution are even more prevalent, that is, to unite myself intimately with Christ, my friend, and to feel more sweetness than can be given by all the earthly joys. It is the joy of feeling yourself intimate with God, even when human beings don't understand you. It is the greatest joy that you can have in your heart.

May 20, 1979

READINGS: ACTS 10:25–26, 34–35, 44–48; 1 JOHN 4:7–10;
JOHN 15:9–17

[198] + THE VOICE OF THE VOICELESS

In whatever political system or situation, the Church should not identify itself with any specific political option. Rather, it supports whatever there is that is just in it, while it is, at the same time, always ready to denounce what is unjust in it. It will not cease being the voice of the voiceless as long as there are people who are oppressed, who are marginalized from participation in the creation and the benefits of the development of the country.

May 20, 1979

[199] + THE GOD OF JESUS CHRIST

God is the God of Jesus Christ. The God of Christians can't be any other; it is the God of Jesus Christ, he who identified himself with the poor, he who gave his life for others. It is the God that sent his Son Jesus Christ to express an unequivocal preference for the poor. Without devaluing others, he called all of them to the side of the poor to be like him. No one is condemned in this life, except only those who reject the call of the humble and poor Christ and whose preference is idolizing wealth and power.

May 27, 1979

READINGS: ACTS 1:1–11; EPHESIANS 1:17–23; MARK 16:15–20

[200] + THE ENVIRONMENT

It is horrifying to hear that the air is being polluted, that there is no water—that there are parts of our capital where there is water for barely a few minutes, and, sometimes, not at all. To hear that the watersheds are drying up, that already those picturesque rivers in our mountains have disappeared. The covenant of humankind with God is not being carried out because humankind is the lord of nature and is becoming the exploiter of nature.

June 3, 1979

READINGS: ACTS 2:1–11; CORINTHIANS 12:3B–7, 12–13; JOHN 20:19–23

[201] + IDOLATRY

How many Christians would be better off not saying that they are Christians because they don't have faith! They have more faith in their money and in their things than in the God that made the things and the money.

June 3, 1979

[202] + THE GOD OF OUR PEOPLE

God is the God of our people, the one who accompanies us in our destiny, the one who accompanies us in our wars and our struggles, the one who accompanies the people in its righteous demands. This marvelous God is the God that we Christians continue to follow. This is the God of revelation, he doesn't need great abstractions or philosophies from Athens. He is not a God of the philosophers. He is the God of whom Christ said, "Father, I give you thanks because you have revealed these things to the simple people, to the humble ones" [Matthew 11:25]. He is the God of the humble ones!

June 10, 1979

READINGS: DEUTERONOMY 4:32–34, 39–40;
ROMANS 8:14–17; MATTHEW 28:16–20

[203] + CHRISTIANITY IS NOT A MUSEUM

It makes me sad to think that there are people who do not grow and change. There are people who say, "Everything that the Church is doing now is bad because it is not the way we did it when we were children." And they remember their school and they want a Christianity that is static as if it were preserved in a museum. Christianity wasn't intended for that, nor was the Gospel. It is to be leavening at the present moment and it has to denounce, not the sins of the time of Moses and Egypt, nor of the time of Christ and of Pilate and of Herod and of the Roman Empire, rather the sins of the present time in El Salvador, those that we are living with, in this historical moment. We have to live this seed of sainthood and unity here in the terrible concrete reality of our people.

June 17, 1979

READINGS: EXODUS 24:3–8; HEBREWS 9:11–15; JOHN 6:51–52

[204] + DIALOGUE

I want to tell you that all of this—is there anyone that doesn't see it?—is symptomatic of a crisis and a structural injustice in our country. Matters cannot be resolved through repression and through violence. It is necessary to enter deeply into a dialogue that is a true dialogue and not a monologue defending only one way of thinking; rather a dialogue in which you are willing to search for the truth and to discard attitudes however cherished they might be. If this doesn't happen, we won't be able to eliminate the roots from which such disagreeable things grow.

June 17, 1979

[205] + THE TRUTH

I have faith, brothers and sisters, that one day all these shadows will be exposed to the light, and that so many disappeared and murdered people, and so many unidentified bodies, and so many kidnappings that we didn't know who did them, will be brought to light. Then, perhaps, we will be amazed to know who the perpetrators were.

June 17, 1979

[206] + THE CHURCH'S SIN

It is time to reflect on the sin of the Church, that any of us could commit, because the one who denounces has to be ready to be denounced. With Christian and evangelical frankness, providing Christians, beginning with myself, an analysis of our behavior faced with the demands of a Church that cannot turn back from its preferential commitment to the poor.

June 21, 1979

[207] + JUDAS'S GESTURE

Also the Mass is prostituted within our Church when it is celebrated with covetousness, when we turned the Mass into commerce. It seems impossible that we would have more Masses only so that we collect more money. It's like what Judas did when he betrayed the Lord for money, and it would be well deserved if the Lord would take up the whip again and say, "My house is a house of prayer and you have made it a den of thieves" [Matthew 21:13].

June 30, 1979

[208] + MARTYRS

Along with the blood of teachers, of workers, of peasants, we can present the blood of our priests. This is a communion of love. It would be sad in a country where there are such horrible assassinations occurring if we could not also count priests among the victims. They are the testimony of a Church incarnate in the problems of the people.

June 30, 1979

[209] + THE EMPIRE OF HELL

Death is a sign of sin, when it produces sin so directly as it does among us: violence, murder, torture where so many are left dead, hacked by machetes, and thrown into the sea. All of this is the empire of hell. Those who kill are of the devil. Those who practice this belong to the devil. They are accomplices, agents of the devil, falsely representing something strange that doesn't fit with God's plan. Because of this, the Church will never tire of denouncing everything that produces death. Death, even natural death, is product and consequence of sin.

July 1, 1979

READINGS: WISDOM 1:13–15, 2:23–25; 2 CORINTHIANS 8:7–9,
13–15; MARK 5:21–43

[210] + THE GOD MOLOCH

They keep on killing teachers. Unidentified bodies keep appearing in different parts of the country. There are so many who have died that it is difficult to list all of them or the political tendency they belonged to. But all of them denounce a macabre dance of vengeance, of institutionalized violence, for some die as direct victims of the repression. Others die precisely because they serve this repression. We can say that our system is like the god Moloch, insatiable in taking victims, be they those who are against him, be they those who serve him. This is how the devil collects. For this reason, when they tell me that I should only pay attention to one kind of dead and not others, I say: any death makes me sorrowful! This macabre dance of death for political vengeance is the best index, a horrific index of how unjust our system is.

July 1, 1979

[211] + THE PREFERENTIAL OPTION
FOR THE POOR

It is a scandal in our atmosphere, which reflects the reality described at Puebla, that there are people and institutions in the Church that are not concerned about the poor and live for their own pleasure. It is necessary, then, that there be an effort at conversion.

July 1, 1979

[212] + CHURCH OF THE POOR

There is a phrase in the greeting of Puebla to the peoples of Latin America that should be the guideline for those that think that when the Church is proclaimed the Church of the poor, it seems that it is becoming partisan and is despising the rich. Not at all! The message is universal. God wants to save the rich, too, but, precisely because he wants to save them, he tells them that they cannot be saved unless they are converted to the Christ that actually lives with the poor. The message of Puebla says that being poor consists of this, "accepting and assuming the cause of the poor, as if you were accepting and assuming it as your own personal cause, the very cause of Christ."

July 1, 1979

[213] + THE RICH

And to the rich I want to say also that a spiritual poverty is not enough, a kind of desire but without effect, to them I say: As long as their desire for evangelical poverty does not become incarnate in the realization that they must take on the cause of the poor as if it were their own cause—as if they were Christ himself—they will continue being called the rich, "those that God despises," because they put more faith in their money.

July 1, 1979

[214] + THE PEOPLE ARE MY PROPHET

The Spirit of Christ has anointed us from the day of our baptism and so we form a people that cannot be mistaken in their belief. What a comfort this is to me, brothers and sisters! You are not wrong when you listen to your bishop and when you come, with a faithfulness that moves me, to the cathedral to hear my poor words. And there is no rejection, on the contrary, I feel that the credibility of the words of your bishop is becoming greater in the hearts of the people. I feel that the people are my prophet.

July 8, 1979

READINGS: EZEKIEL 2:2–5; 2 CORINTHIANS 12:7–10; MARK 6:1–6

[215] + GOD'S MICROPHONES

Each one of you has to be God's microphone. Each one of you has to be a messenger, a prophet. The Church will always exist as long as there is someone who has been baptized, even if there is only one person baptized in the whole world, this person has the responsibility to the world to make sure the flag of the Lord's truth and his divine justice continues to fly. Because of this, it is painful to think of the cowardice of so many Christians and in the betrayal of others who have been baptized. What are you doing, those of you who are baptized, in the world of politics? Where is your baptism? You are baptized in your professions, in the fields of workers, in the market. Wherever there is someone who has been baptized, that is where the Church is. There is a prophet there. This is where you have to say something in the name of the truth that shines on the lies of the earth. Let us not be cowards. Let us not hide the talent that God gave us on the day of our baptism and let us truly live the beauty and responsibility of being a prophetic people.

July 8, 1979

[216] + PROPHETIC PEOPLE

Those who laugh at me, as if I were crazy to think that I am a prophet, ought to reflect on this. I have never considered myself a prophet in the sense of being unique among the people, because I know that you and I, the people of God, are a prophetic people. And my role in this is only to stimulate a prophetic sense in the people. This is something I can't give them, rather it is the Spirit that has given it to them. And each one of you can say truly, "The Spirit came upon me when I was baptized and it sent me to the Salvadoran society, to the people of El Salvador," which today is having such a hard time because the prophetic mission has failed in many who were baptized. But, thank God, I also want to say that there is in our archdiocese a prophetic awakening in the Christian Base Communities, in this group that reflects on the Word of God, in this critical consciousness that is being formed in our Christianity that no longer wants a Christianity of the masses but rather a conscious Christianity; one in which before being baptized, there is study of the catechism, in which before getting married there is instruction so one understands what one is committing to and to truly be the honor of this people of God. I am glad, and I want to congratulate the Church of the archdiocese in these efforts to awaken the prophetic sense of our Christians. This charism will never be lacking in us.

July 8, 1979

[217] + RELIGION NEEDS PROPHETS

Prophets also denounce internal sins of the Church. And why shouldn't they? Bishops, the pope, priests, papal nuncios, women religious, Catholic schools, are formed by men and women, and men and women are sinners and need a prophet to call us to conversion, so that we don't establish religion as if it were unchangeable. Religion needs prophets; thank God that we have them. Because it would be very sad if a church felt that it was in possession of the truth and rejected everything else. A church that only condemns, a church that only looks at the sin in others and doesn't see the beam that it has in its eye, is not the authentic Church of God.

July 8, 1979

[218] + THE PROPHET'S SUCCESS

The prophet's success is not when the people that hear his preaching are converted; if this happens, blessed be God. God has achieved his ends through this instrument. But if the prophet doesn't manage to convert this stubborn people, it doesn't matter. Success consists in this: that a stubborn, sinful, unfaithful people, at least recognizes that there was a prophet who spoke to them in the name of God.

July 8, 1979

[219] + DOGS THAT DON'T BARK

The prophet's mission is terrible: The prophet must speak even knowing that people are not going to listen. If people don't listen, they will be lost through their own fault, but the prophet has carried out his responsibility. There were those who said, "The Lord says this." And if, thank God, the evildoers heard the prophet, they will be saved and it will also be glory to the prophet that preached to them. We cannot remain silent, dear brothers and sisters, as a prophetic Church in such a corrupt, unjust world. It would truly be the incarnation of that terrible image of dogs that don't bark. What use is a dog that doesn't bark, that doesn't take care of the property it is supposed to guard?

July 8, 1979

[220] + PROPHETIC CHURCH

Many people in high places and who think themselves the owners of the Church, think that the Church has abandoned them and that the Church has forgotten its spiritual mission. They think that it no longer preaches spirituality, that it only preaches politics. That's not true, it is pointing out our sin and this society has to listen to this and be converted to be what God wants.

July 8, 1979

[221] + FREEDOM AND SLAVERY

No one is so free as the one who is not under the yoke of the god money. And no one is so enslaved as the one who idolizes money.

July 15, 1979

READINGS: AMOS 7:12–15; EPHESIANS 1:3–14; MARK 6:7–13

[222] + MONEY AND PROGRESS

Money is necessary for peoples to progress, we aren't going to deny that. But a progress like ours, which depends on the exploitation of so many who will never enjoy the progress of our society, is not evangelical poverty. What good are our beautiful highways and airport, beautiful multi-storied buildings if they are only built with the blood of poor people who will never be able to enjoy them?

July 15, 1979

[223] + SPIRITUALITY OF THE POOR

No one understands the poor as well as one who is evangelically poor. Such persons know what the hunger of a mother, of a child, of people living in a shack is like, because they also live it, perhaps not in identical physical conditions, but in the spirituality of the poor that makes them able to understand and share it. Such people don't give as from one above to one below; now is not the time for paternalism; it is a time for brotherhood and sisterhood, of feeling that one is brother or sister, that what is important to the poor, to the peasant, to the have-nots, is important to me.

July 15, 1979

[224] + THE PERSECUTED CHURCH

And I am glad, brothers and sisters, that our Church is perse-cuted precisely because of its preferential option for the poor and because it tries to become incarnate in the interests of the poor and say to all the people, those who govern, the rich and the powerful: If you do not become poor, if you do not take an interest in the poverty of the people as if they were your own family, you will not be able to save society.

July 15, 1979

[225] + VICTIMS OF CONSUMER SOCIETY

If there is a sickness in the poor and from the middle class on down, it is the most terrible sickness: to be the victims of consumer society. Wanting to have your television set right now, wanting also to have your receptions like those in the higher classes, wanting to enjoy life even without having the minimum for survival. The spirit of poverty is the best way to avoid these temptations that destroy the family and human happiness.

July 15, 1979

[226] + THE POOR CHURCH

v wise Jesus Christ is to say to the apostles that they should go spread the Gospel using the figure of the poor pilgrim! And today's Church has to be converted to this commandment of Christ. Now is not the time for fancy clothes, for big useless buildings, for the great pomp of our Church. All of this perhaps had a purpose in its time and we have to continue with it in the function of evangelization and of service. But now, more than ever, the Church wants to present itself as poor among the poor and poor among the rich, to evangelize both the poor and the rich.

July 15, 1979

[227] + A LIBERATING DEVOTION

If tomorrow, feast day of the Virgin of El Carmen, the crowds run to her image and wear scapulars, don't forget that Mary is, above all, a prophetic messenger of Christ and that in her song of the Magnificat she remembered the poor and the hungry. She also said that God would ask for an accounting from the proud and the haughty, from the rich people of the world and warned that he would turn them away empty if they were not converted to the poverty of God.... Have great devotion to the Virgin, but, brothers and sisters, a liberating devotion, a devotion that enables us to learn from Mary the freedom with which she spoke. A devotion to the Virgin that makes us feel ourselves face to face with God, not to implant our way of thinking or our false prudence, but rather so that we can know how to put ourselves on the line for Christ, when, because of the injustice of the world, he is nailed on the cross. When everyone else flees, she remains there near him.

July 15, 1979

[228] + FALSE PROPHETS

How terrible it is when the priestly or prophetic mission is subordinated to economic considerations, when the prophetic and priestly ministry is carried out in subordination to these social and economic interests! How many times, dear brothers and sisters—and I am speaking of you the laity who are the prophetic people of God—once you manage to reach a political post you are no longer the same as you were before. How many betrayals have we had to lament!

July 15, 1979

[229] + PROPHETIC CHURCH

We shouldn't try to please those in high places. We have to say our word in the name of God, denouncing so much injustice. There are so many ways to become accomplices of the criminal hands! The Church cannot get involved in all of this; it has to speak out even when it may offend those who, like Amaziah, have to make the voice of their king more respected than the message of their God.

July 15, 1979

[230] + PERSONAL AND SOCIAL SIN

To wish to speak of confessing sin only so that you not have individual sin, and, at the same time not struggling against the injustice that is around you, is not being the true people of God. Along with striving not to have personal sin, it is necessary also to struggle against the power of hell and the devil to eliminate the social sins and their root causes.

July 15, 1979

[231] + PRAYER

Praying and expecting everything to come from God and not doing anything yourself is not praying. This is laziness; this is alienation. This is passivity, conformity. This is not the time, dear brothers and sisters to say: It is God's will. Many things that happen are not God's will. When people can contribute something of themselves to improve the situation and ask God for the courage to do so, then that is prayer.

July 29, 1979

READINGS: 2 KINGS 4:42–44; EPHESIANS 4:1–6; JOHN 6:1–15

[232] + BEING THE VOICE OF THE VOICELESS

A reporter either tells the truth or is not really a reporter. For this reason, I want to thank the Independent Journalists Agency, API, which has been so kind as to pick up my homily from last week and give it ample coverage. I think there are four whole pages, something extraordinary, since we can say that no one is a prophet in his own land. When I see my modest homilies even published in English, in French, outside the country, and they send them to me, I don't see an echo in the press of this country of what we were saying earlier, that they ought to give witness to the truth. These homilies are trying to be the voice of this people, the voice of the voiceless. And, because of this, those with too much voice don't like them. This poor voice will find echo in those who, as I said before, love the truth and truly love our dear people.

July 29, 1979

[233] + GOD DOESN'T WANT DISPERSION

God is also careful to protect the justice of the demands of the organizations that have the right to organize for the mutual defense of their rights. God also approves of efforts to build unions. God wants humankind to be united. God does not want us to be dispersed. God wants—as the pope has said—for peasants to be able to join together with other peasants and not be separated so that they might be an easily exploitable mass.

August 5, 1979
READINGS: EXODUS 16:2–4, 12–15; EPHESIANS 4:17, 20–24;
JOHN 6:24–35

[234] + MAKING RICHES ABSOLUTE

Above all, I denounce making riches an absolute. This is the greatest ill of El Salvador: wealth and private property as an untouchable absolute and, woe be to those who touch this high-tension wire. They will get burned! It is not justice for a few to have everything and to make this absolute in such a way that no one can touch it, while the marginalized majority is dying of hunger.

August 12, 1979
READINGS: 1 KINGS 19:4–8; EPHESIANS 4:30—5:2; JOHN 6:41–51

[235] + YOU ALL ARE THE TEMPLE

Without Christ the temples mean nothing however beautiful they may be.... One of our popular composers, singing about the death of Father Rafael Palacios [murdered in June], says this beautiful phrase, "God is not in the temple but rather in the community." You all are the temple! What good is it that we have beautiful churches if Christ could say of them what he says today to the Pharisees, "Your worship is empty." There may be much luxurious worship, with many flowers, with many things, guests and everything, but where is the adoration in Spirit and in truth?

September 2, 1979

[*Note:* The song is by Guillermo Cuéllar.]

READINGS: DEUTERONOMY 4:1–2, 6–8;
JAMES 1:17–18, 21B–22, 27; MARK 7:1–8A, 14–15, 21–23

[236] + WE HAVE BECOME COMMERCIALIZED

Perhaps, with my brother priests, we have made worship consist of decorating the altar beautifully and, perhaps, raising the fees to be able decorate it even better. We have become commercialized! Because of this, God is saying to us, as if he were entering Jerusalem with a whip, "You have made my house a den of thieves" [Matthew 21:13].

September 2, 1979

[237] + TRUE AND FALSE RELIGION

Be careful! Don't make your religion consist only of theoretical things. If a religion is lacking in works, it won't get you into the kingdom of heaven. The Lord has already said it: It is not the one who says Lord, Lord, the one who prays a great deal with beautiful prayers, who will enter the kingdom of heaven. It is rather the one who does the will of my Father in heaven. This is the true religion: not just remaining pure, but visiting widows and orphans. This is a biblical expression that means to concern yourself with those in need.

September 2, 1979

[238] + PATERNALISM

We don't serve the poor with paternalism, helping him or her as if reaching down from above to someone below. This is not what God wants, but rather he wants us to do this as one brother or sister to another. This is my brother or sister, this is Christ; and, with Christ, I am not reaching down from above to someone below, rather I am reaching up from below, to serve him above.

September 2, 1979

[239] + WHAT POWER DOES DEATH
HAVE OVER ME?

For myself, dear brothers and sisters, I wouldn't want to have a life like that of many of the powerful today, who don't really live. They are surrounded by guards; they live with uneasy consciences, in anxiety. This is not living! "If you carry out the law of God, you will live." Although they may kill me, I do not need.... If we die with a clear conscience, with a clean heart because we have done only good works, then what power does death have over us? Thank God that we have these examples of our beloved pastoral agents, who shared the dangers of our pastoral work, even the risk of being killed. When I celebrate the Eucharist with you, I feel their presence. Each priest that is killed is, for me, a new concelebrant of the Eucharist of our archdiocese. I know that they are here giving us the inspiration of having known how to die unafraid, because their consciences were committed to the law of the Lord: to the preferential option for the poor.

September 2, 1979

[240] + PREFERENTIAL OPTION FOR THE POOR

It is inconceivable that someone is called "Christian" and does not make a preferential option for the poor as Christ did. It is a scandal that today's Christians criticize the Church because it is concerned with the poor.

September 9, 1979

READINGS: ISAIAH 35:4–7A; JAMES 2:1–5; MARK 7:31–37

[241] + INDIVIDUALISTIC EDUCATION

Sadly, dear brothers and sisters, we are the product of a spiritualistic, individualistic education, in which they have taught us, "Worry about saving your own soul and don't worry about anyone else." We have said to those who are suffering, "Patience, heaven will come. Endure." No! It can't be this way. This is not saving; it is not the salvation that Christ brought. The salvation that Christ brought is salvation from all the kinds of slavery that oppress humankind.... It is necessary that the person of today who lives under the sign of so many different kinds of oppression and slavery— fear that enslaves hearts, illness that oppresses our bodies, sadness, worry, the terror that oppresses our liberty and our life—break all these chains. We have to begin here!

September 9, 1979

[242] + THE BISHOP ALWAYS HAS A GREAT DEAL TO LEARN FROM HIS PEOPLE

This is how we can know who are authentic Catholics: They are united with their bishop. If they are not with the bishop, they cannot call themselves good Catholics. This doesn't mean that the bishop is a despot, "do what I say." Because the service the bishop does is precisely to serve the people. Specifically in this meeting in which I spoke of the *Cursillos* of Christianity, we had such a profound reflection that I think that the bishop always has a great deal to learn from his people. It is precisely in the charisms that the Spirit gives people, that the bishop finds the touchstone of his humility and of his authenticity. I want to thank all of those who, when they don't agree with the bishop, have the courage to enter into dialogue with him and either to convince him of his error or be convinced of their error.

September 9, 1979

[243] + ORGANIZATION

I would like to issue a call now to my dear Christians: you are not forbidden to organize; it is a right, and, at some moments, like today, it is also an obligation, because political and social demands have to be achieved, not by isolated people, but rather through the strength of a people that join together to demand their just rights. The sin is not in organizing; sin is, for a Christian, to lose the perspective of God.

September 16, 1979

READINGS: ISAIAH 50:5–10; JAMES 2:14–18; MARK 8:27–35

[244] + NO LONGER CHRISTIANS

Christians that are in solidarity with the forces of oppression are not true Christians. Christians who defend unjust positions that are indefensible, only to keep their status, are no longer Christians.

September 16, 1979

[245] + A CHILD'S SMILE

A child's smile is worth millions. How much more valuable is it to me that a child has enough confidence in me to smile at me, to hug me, and even to give me a kiss when leaving the church, than if I had millions and children were scared of me.

September 23, 1979

READINGS: WISDOM 2:17–20; JAMES 3:16–18, 4:1–3; MARK 9:29–36

[246] + TRANSCENDENCE

The transcendence that the Church preaches is not alienation; it is not going to heaven to think about eternal life and forget about the problems on earth. It's a transcendence from the human heart. It is entering into the reality of a child, of the poor, of those wearing rags, of the sick, of a hovel, of a shack. It is going to share with them. And from the very heart of misery, of this situation, to transcend it, to elevate it, to promote it, to say to them, "You aren't trash. You aren't marginalized." It is to say exactly the opposite, "You are valuable."

September 23, 1979

[*Note:* Romero is here quoting from his Fourth Pastoral Letter.]

[247] + WE HAVE TO HONOR THEIR MEMORY

Why do they kill priests? They kill them because they find them bothersome. For me, they are true martyrs in the popular sense. Naturally, I am not talking about the canonical sense where being a martyr supposes a process of the supreme authority of the Church, which proclaims them martyrs of the universal Church. I respect this law and will never say that our assassinated priests are martyrs that are already canonized. But, yes, they are martyrs in the popular sense, they are men who have preached precisely this identification with the poor. They are true men who have gone to the limits of danger where they are threatened by the UGB, where someone can be pointed out and end up being killed as they killed Christ. These are the ones that I call truly just. And if they had their blemishes, who doesn't, brothers and sisters? What human beings don't have anything to be sorry about? The priests who have been killed are also men and had their blemishes. But because they let themselves be killed and didn't run away, because they were not cowards and put themselves in this situation of torture, of suffering, of murder, this is, for me, as valuable as a baptism of blood and they have been purified. We have to honor their memory.

September 23, 1979

[Note: The UGB is the Unión Guerrera Blanca, the White Warriors Union. Jim Brockman says in his biography of Romero that "Like similar names used by the violent right, the White Warriors Union seems to have no history or identifiable members... Rightist groups were phantomlike, and to many they seemed to be simple names used by the secruty forces to disguise some of their actions" (56). It is believed that they generated the handbills which said: "Be a Patriot, Kill a Priest." In May of 1977, they declared they had killed the young priest

Fr. Alfonso Navarro in retaliation for the death of the kidnapped foreign minister Mauricio Borgonovo. In June, they announced that unless the Jesuits left the country within 21 days, they and their institutions would become "military targets." In September of 1979, Romero received a threat from them through the mail in an official envelope from the Defense Ministry.]

[248] + KNOWING HOW TO LISTEN

If I were a jealous person like the people in the Gospel and the first reading, I would say, "Forbid [him]. Don't let him speak, don't let him say anything. Only I, the bishop, can speak" [see Numbers 11:28]. No. I have to listen to what the Spirit says through the people and, then, yes, receive this message from the people and analyze it and together with the people build the Church.

September 30, 1979

READINGS: NUMBERS 11:25–29; JAMES 5:1–6;

MARK 9:37–42, 44, 46–47

[249] + PRIVATE PROPERTY

A restructuring of our economic and social systems is needed because there shouldn't be this absolutizing, this idolatry of private property, which, frankly, is a form of paganism. The Christian cannot accept private property as an absolute.

September 30, 1979

[250] + CHRIST PRESENT IN THE LITTLE ONES

And we return here to the preferential option for the poor. It is not demagoguery; it is pure Gospel. If we don't concern ourselves about the interests of the poor, of the littlest ones, and not in just any way but because they represent Jesus, because of the faith that the humble, the marginalized, the poor and the sick open up to us, and because we see Jesus in them. This is transcendence. When we only see a competitor, someone who has been unwise, someone who exists to spoil our fun, then, naturally, the poor bother us. But when we embrace them, as Christ embraced the leper and as the good Samaritan lifted up the wounded man from the road—because what we do for another, we do for Christ— this is transcendence without which the social justice perspective is not possible. Christ is present in the little ones.

September 30, 1979

[251] + MATRIMONY

No one gets married just so that the two of them can be happy. Marriage has a great social function; it has to be a torch that lights the area around it, other marriages, paths to other liberations. The man and the woman have to leave their homes, later they are able to promote the changes that are needed in politics, in society, in the paths of justice—changes that won't be made as long as the homes are opposed to them. On the contrary, it will be very easy when little girls and boys are being formed in the bosom of each family who will not desire so much to have more, rather to be more, not by acquiring everything but in giving with full hands to others. You have to be taught to love. The family is nothing but love and love is giving oneself; love is giving oneself to the well being of all. It is working for common happiness.

October 7, 1979

READINGS: GENESIS 2:18–24; HEBREWS 2:9–11; MARK 10:2–6

[252] + IT IS NOT ENOUGH TO BE GOOD

Here there is a challenge from Christ to the goodness of humankind. It is not enough to be good. It is not enough to not do evil. My Christianity is something more positive; it is not a negative. There are many who say, "But I don't kill, I don't steal, I don't do anything bad to anyone." That's not enough. You are still lacking a great deal.

October 14, 1979

READINGS: WISDOM 7:7–11; HEBREWS 4:12–13; MARK 10:17–30

[253] + CHURCH AND GOVERNMENT

If there is a conflict between the government and the Church, it is not because the Church is a political opponent of the government. It is rather because the conflict is already established between the government and the people, and the Church defends the people.

October 21, 1979

READINGS: ISAIAH 53:10–11; HEBREWS 4:14–16; MARK 10:35–45

[254] + THE CHURCH AND THE KINGDOM OF GOD

This is my principal wish as pastor, for us to affirm the Church through building the kingdom of God. And to do this in such a way that the Church does not seek conflict with anyone nor to flatter anyone, but rather to be herself. Those who, as she does, struggle to bring the kingdom of God on earth will get along with the Church; and those who are opposed to the kingdom of God on earth will be in conflict with the Church.

October 28, 1979

READINGS: JEREMIAH 31:7–9, HEBREWS 5:1–6; MARK 14:46–52

[255] + ORGANIZATION

We have said a thousand times that the Church defends the right of the people to organize. But even beginning with very noble ends, this also can be prostituted in a false adoration when it becomes an absolute, when organization is considered as the supreme value and all other interests are already subordinated to it, even though they come from the people. The people don't matter any longer, just the organization.

November 4, 1979

READINGS: DEUTERONOMY 6:2–6; HEBREWS 7:23–28;

MARK 12:28–34

[256] + IMPUNITY

Evil exists; it is necessary that these members of the security forces be aware that many times they have acted under orders and that if there is a purge of the security forces, the ones who should be judged and punished are the commanders who have corrupted the minds of these men.

November 4, 1979

[257] + THE DO-GOODERS

There are little parties many times for Christmas or birthdays with piñatas. Those who give one of these little parties think they are doing something great, yet they don't pay their workers a just wage. They want to give as charity what they already owe in justice.

November 11, 1979

READINGS: 1 KINGS 17:10–16; HEBREWS 9:24–28; MARK 12:38–44

[258] + THE POOR

The poor are the ones who are forging our history.

November 11, 1979

[259] + PROGRESS

Only the one who has poverty of spirit will know how to put God and humankind, which is the key to all of civilization, above all else. It is not having big buildings, having huge airports, super highways, if only a privileged minority will be able to use them and not the people with whose blood all these things were built.

November 11, 1979

[260] + WHEN THE POOR BELIEVE IN THE POOR

No one understands the poor as well as another who also is poor.

November 11, 1979

[261] + IDOLATRY OF MONEY

I repeat, to those who are still on their knees to their money, figure out how to separate yourselves from it out of love before it is torn from you by violence. This is the danger of the extreme right. And not just of the extreme right, but of everybody. My vision is a pastoral one; it is the Word of the Gospel that I am preaching. From Christ, I say that the great danger to true civilization is the uncontrolled love of earthly goods. The example of these two widows and the prophet Elias are eloquent calls from God at a crucial time for El Salvador. They are calls to cut yourself loose in order to be free, and with a free heart, to work for the true liberation of our people.

November 11, 1979

[262] + THE CHURCH AND THE RICH

The other day, we asked one of the men that proclaims liberation in a political sense, "What does the Church mean to you?" And he said this scandalous thing, "There are actually two Churches: the Church of the poor and the church of the rich. We believe in the Church of the poor, but we don't believe in the church of the rich." Of course, this phrase is demagoguery and I will never say that there is a division in the Church. There is only one Church, the one that Christ preaches. This is the Church that has to give itself with all of its heart. Those who call themselves Catholic and yet adore their riches and don't want to let go of them are not Christian; they have not understood the call of the Lord. This is not church. The rich people kneeling down before their money, even though these people may go to Mass and even though they might do pious acts, if they have not turned away from the idol money in their hearts, they are idolaters; they are not Christians. There is only one Church, the one that adores the true God and the one that knows how to give each thing its proper value.

November 11, 1979

[263] + THERE IS NO MORE HORRIBLE SCANDAL

How shameful when the religious service becomes a way to earn money! There is no more horrible scandal. And I would say to my dear brother priests, and to the Catholic institutions, to the congregations and the schools, and to all those that call themselves—and want to be—Church: Be careful not to fall into what Christ severely criticized, contrasted with the authentic devotion of the widow, that is, the attitude of the falsely religious that turn the evil intentions they harbor inside into pomposity and externalities.

November 11, 1979

[264] + PRAYER

Because of this, I insist on much prayer. Let us pray, but not with the kind of prayer that alienates us, not with a kind of prayer that makes us avoid reality. We should never go to church as a flight from our duties on earth. Let's go to church to get strength and clarity to return to better carry out our tasks at home, our political duties, our tasks in the organization. This is a healthy orientation to these things of earth. These are the true liberators.

November 11, 1979

[265] + I WILL NOT ABANDON MY PEOPLE

I want to clarify one point. The news of death threats to my person have been much repeated.... I want to assure you, and I ask your prayers that I be faithful to this promise, that I will not abandon my people, rather I will run the same risks with them that my ministry requires.

November 11, 1979

[266] + WITH THIS PEOPLE IT IS NOT HARD TO BE A GOOD SHEPHERD

With this people it is not hard to be a good shepherd. This is a people that compels to its service those of us who have been called to defend its rights and to be its voice.

November 18, 1979

READINGS: DANIEL 12:1–3; HEBREWS 10:11–14, 18; MARK 13:24–32

[267] + THE TRUTH

Let us not be afraid to stand alone if it is a result of honoring truth. Let us be afraid of being demagogues and desiring to receive false adulation from the people. If we don't tell the truth, we are committing the worse sin. We are betraying the truth and betraying the people.

November 25, 1979

READINGS: DANIEL 7:13–14; REVELATION 1:5–8; JOHN 18:33–37

[268] + SOCIAL INJUSTICE

And if we are talking about justice and finding the causes of our problems, I think the new government ought not to rest until it finds the root cause, which is social injustice. We have always thought that all the violence done by the security forces—or that the security forces have suffered—has something even more criminal behind it: social injustice.

November 25, 1979

[269] + PROGRESS

What is the purpose of progress? It is not for a few to have everything and others nothing, rather progress is so that the truth of Christ, which is salvation, reaches everyone. Also, the pope has told us that the criterion for all these relationships is humankind. The criterion of justice that must prevail will not be to guarantee that one can keep what one has acquired, rather to be vigilant so that the riches of society and even private property, carry out their social function; that the properties allow for satisfying the basic necessities of all Salvadorans.

December 9, 1979

READINGS: BARUCH 5:1–9; PHILIPPIANS 1:4–6, 8–11; LUKE 3:1–6

[270] + STRUCTURE OF JUSTICE

The need for structures for justice, for distribution, better than those that are dominant, always comes up. It is urgent, and I hope that those in the government will be strong in this and make these changes in spite of all their hat-waving and the threats of the monied class. I hope that they don't stop the way that previous regimes did which saw the need for structural change but didn't dare do it because the power of money was greater than the will of the government. I would hope that the principal concern of ANEP and of all those that defend its interests were not to maintain their position but rather to see how the country's economy would permit all Salvadorans to sustain their families with the fruits of their labor, in a dignified way. This is the ideal that between all of us we must work for.

December 9, 1979

[Note: ANEP refers to Asociación Nacional de la Empresa Privada, the National Association of Private Enterprise.]

[271] + THE PARTICIPATION OF WOMEN IN POLITICS

Don't forget that the pope said the participation of women in politics is valid but that it must be critical participation. Women must not allow themselves to be used for the benefit of certain interests, especially if they are selfish ones. Let women be critical in their analysis of what to participate in and what not to participate in. The Salvadoran woman has always been very dignified. I hope she will honor her tradition and not allow herself to be used, especially against her will.

December 9, 1979

[272] + THEY TRAMPLED ON THE CONSTITUTION

It is urgent to streamline the process so that in a relatively short time we will see concrete results in the solution of these problems so felt by the people. I believe that this is being tied up to a great extent in legalisms and legalities. Why didn't they talk so much before about respect for the Constitution? They trampled on the Constitution like they wanted to and now that it has to do precisely with reestablishing respect for human rights, it shouldn't be the laws that impede this process of the dignity of man. I want to remind you here of that great phrase of Jesus Christ when he spoke of the Sabbath, "Man is not made for the law, but the law for man." And I hope that we have a government that will take action, real steps, that will not get so embroiled in legalism so that peace might return to this country quickly.

December 9, 1979

[273] + DOCTOR HONORIS CAUSA

I want to end by expressing my appreciation for the congratulations sent me because of the degree of Doctor Honoris Causa that will be conferred on me by the University of Louvain next February 2. As I have said on numerous occasions: I don't feel that all these honors are mine, nor do they puff me up with pride, rather they give me the joy of sharing with you, dear brothers and sisters, a pastoral line of defense of the Gospel of human dignity and the rights of man. And it is you who are also honored along with me with all these awards. And it is in your name that I will go accept this award, God willing.

December 9, 1979

[274] + GOD IS AMONG US

No Christians should feel alone on their path, no family has to feel abandoned, no people should be pessimistic even amid crises that seem insoluble, like those of our country. God is among us. Let us have faith in this central truth of the sacred revelation. God is present; he is not asleep, rather, he is active, he observes, he helps and, at the proper time, he will act appropriately. Because of this, the presence of God awakens true joy in our hearts: Rejoice in the Lord! Again I say to you: Rejoice because God is near!

December 16, 1979

READINGS: ZEPHANIAH 3:14–18A; PHILIPPIANS 4:4–7;
LUKE 3:10–18

[275] + GOD IS JOY

God is joy, God doesn't want sadness, God is optimistic, God is the possibility of everything good, God is all-powerful to do good and to love. Who can be sad given a God whose presence fills everything.

December 16, 1979

[276] + GOD DOES NOT WANT SOCIAL INJUSTICE

Redemption has been carried out on the cross; the pain of human-kind is the cross and as the cross it brings redemption, and should give peace, Easter joy, and hope of resurrection. It is not conformity because conformity is not joy. Conformity is a pessimistic person, a deterministic person that believes that everything is imposed on him from above and that he cannot take any action. This is a false concept— I would call it blasphemy—of the will of God. People who don't want to end their situation of oppression, their situation of marginalization thinking that this is the will of God, are offending God. God does not want social injustice!

December 16, 1979

[277] + TRUE POVERTY

True poverty is to concern ourselves preferentially with the poor as if it were our own cause. And, because of this, it is also to feel that one is poor and needs strength from God in all situations.

December 16, 1979

[278] + THE CHURCH DOES NOT SELL OUT TO ANYONE

The Church does not sell out to anyone; the Church is committed only to the kingdom of God and makes the same demands as the kingdom on everyone who draws near. It must not reject anyone who seeks it with a sincere heart.

December 16, 1979

[279] + A SINCERE SOLIDARITY

A person who has two tunics, give one to someone who doesn't have any; a person who has enough to eat, share even the little that you have. This is a society in solidarity; this is the solidarity that the Church promotes, concerned with giving everyone what they need and not blindly accepting differences born of money or of force. "Don't abuse people" [Luke 3:14], John the Baptist said, and the Church repeats, "Don't abuse." There are not two categories of people. There are not some who were born to have everything and leave others with nothing and a majority that has nothing and can't enjoy the happiness that God has created for all. God wants a Christian society, one in which we share the good things that God has given for all of us.

December 16, 1979

[280] + A CRITICAL SENSE

I want to insist on this, brothers and sisters, because I believe that what a mature Salvadoran needs most today is a critical sense. Don't wait to see which way the bishop leans, or what others say, or what the organization says. Each one of you has to be a critical man, a critical woman. "The tree is known by its fruits." But be sure that you act and criticize based on their actions: the government, the popular political organization, the political parties, group X. Don't let yourselves be carried along, don't let yourselves be manipulated. You are the ones, the people, who have to give the verdict of justice as to what the people need.

December 16, 1979

[281] + CONVERSION OF THE RICH

Rich people must criticize their own surroundings
person: why they have wealth, and why there are so many, poor
people around them. If these people are rich Christians, they
will find in this personal critique the beginning of their conversion: Why am I rich and why are there so many people who are
hungry around me?

December 16, 1979

[282] + MACHISMO

The unfaithful spouse will be converted and will become a model
spouse when he becomes aware of his machismo and why he is
not able to have an adult, mature, Christian relationship with his
wife.

December 16, 1979

[283] + I OFFER YOU SOME REFLECTIONS HERE

I offer you some reflections here on the Word of God with the
aim that each one of you assimilate this and from your own
personality act as a Christian if you truly want to honor the faith
that you profess and not be subject to manipulation nor become
a victim of the atmosphere around you.

December 16, 1979

[284] + PROSTITUTION

The conversion of a publican is not enough, or of a soldier, or of an alcoholic. We must uncover the network of complicity that permits the existence of large-scale prostitution. The fact is that it has become a system! And when we are told who the owners are of certain motels and certain whorehouses, we are horrified! Sometimes, the same puritans who condemn the immorality of the people form part of this system: corrupting the people with drunkenness and prostitution.

December 16, 1979

[285] + TRUE CONVERSION

A true Christian conversion today has to uncover the social mechanisms that make the worker or the peasant marginalized people. Why is there income for the poor peasant only during the harvests of coffee, cotton, or sugar cane? Why does this society need peasants without work, badly paid workers, people without just salaries? These mechanisms must be brought to light, not in the way that we study sociology or economy, but rather as Christians, in order to not be complicit in this machinery that is creating ever poorer, marginalized, and indigent people.

December 16, 1979

[286] + POPULAR ORGANIZATIONS

I feel that as pastor I have a duty to the popular political organizations. Even when they distrust me, my duty is to defend their right to organize, to support everything just in their demands. But also, I want to maintain my autonomy to criticize any abuses in their organization, anything that means idolizing the organization; and to call them, rather, to a dialogue of true seeking of solutions among all of us. The organized forces are powerful in a society and can do anything when they are able to dialogue. But they also lose strength when they become fanatic and only want to hear their own voices. The voice of the archbishop, then, is not a systematic opposition to the organizations.

December 16, 1979

[287] + AGRARIAN REFORM

It is not that the Junta has the right to carry out an agrarian reform, it has the obligation to do so! The words of John Paul II are a slogan: to remove from the peasants and the poor the barriers of exploitation. It also seems to me to be important for the current government to carry out reforms, not as a gift that the Junta gives the people in order to gain their support. The agrarian reform is a conquest that the people have earned with their blood that has been shed.... The agrarian reform should not be carried out with the intention of finding a way out for the capitalist model that would allow it to continue developing and continue to accumulate and concentrate riches in only a few hands, whether in the industrial, commercial or financial sector. Nor should it be done to pacify the peasants and keep them from continuing to organize and increase their political, economic and social participation. The agrarian reform should not make the peasants dependent on the State, rather it should leave them free in reference to the State.... The Salvadoran agrarian reform should have an ample vision: not just looking toward redistribution of land, but of all the social resources. So that all peasants and poor might have: doctors, schools, hospitals, electricity, water, etc. In a word, to move toward integral human development.

December 16, 1979

[288] + A CALL TO THE OLIGARCHY

I also want to address myself in this moment and matter which is so serious and sensitive to the economically powerful sectors that will be affected by the agrarian reform. I want to speak to you, dear brothers and sisters, not as judge or as enemy, but rather as pastor and as a Salvadoran brother of all the Salvadorans. I want to invite you to realize what a great responsibility you have at this moment, to collaborate so that the economic, social, and political crisis of this country be overcome without resorting to violence. These demonstrations of gunfire and, especially, creating fear among the people—if it is not true—that the right is bringing arms into the country and is hiring mercenaries, are not the way to defend your well being.

December 16, 1979

[289] + THAT IS NOT WHERE GOD IS

t, let us not look for God in the opulence of the world, in idolatry of riches, in the desire for power, in intrigues of the great. That's not where God is. Let us look for God with the sign of the angels: lying in a manger, wrapped in the poor swaddling clothes that a humble peasant from Nazareth could provide for him, some poor cloths and a little hay as the resting place of the God that was made man, of the King of the centuries made accessible to people as a poor little child. It is time to look today at baby Jesus, but not in the beautiful images of our mangers. We have to look for him among the malnourished children that went to bed tonight without having had anything to eat, among the poor newspaper vendors that will sleep wrapped in papers in the doorways, among the poor shoe shine boys that perhaps have earned enough to take a small gift to their mothers, or, who knows, the newspaper vendors that didn't manage to sell all of their papers and will receive a tremendous reprimand from their stepfather or stepmother. How sad is the story of our children! Jesus takes on all of this tonight.

December 24, 1979

[290] + THERE IS NO REDEMPTION WITHOUT THE CROSS

Not everything is joy, there is much suffering, there are many homes that have been destroyed, there is much pain and there is much poverty. Brothers and sisters, we are not looking at all of this with demagoguery. The God of the poor has assumed all of this and he is teaching human pain the redemptive value, the value that it has to redeem the world of poverty, suffering, the cross. There is no redemption without the cross. But this doesn't mean a passivity on the part of our poor, of those we have badly indoctrinated when we say to them, "It is the will of God that you are poor, marginalized and that you have no hope." This is not true! God does not want this social injustice; but, once it exists it means a great sin of the oppressors—and their greatest violence is that they deprive so many human beings of happiness and that they are killing with hunger so many who are malnourished. God demands justice but he is saying to the poor, as Christ did to the oppressed, by carrying your cross, you will save the world if you don't accept your suffering out of a conformity that is not God's will. Rather be concerned with salvation, dying in your poverty desiring better times, making of your life a prayer and accepting everything that tries to free the people from this situation.

December 24, 1979

[291] + SIN OF OMISSION

What can I do and what didn't I do? What did I do wrong? Because I am the first to recognize that, as all limited human beings, not everything that I have done is good. That when I ask the Lord in the Mass to pardon me for sins of omission, I am indicating the most mysterious chapter of the evil in each heart: what we could have done and didn't. How much of a hole do we leave in life, how much good do we refrain from doing!

December 31, 1979

[292] + THE STRENGTH THAT MUST SUSTAIN US

We want to say to all Salvadorans that it is true that we live in very uncertain times. What awaits us in 1980? Will it be the year of a civil war? Will it be the year of total destruction? Will we not have merited compassion from God because of so much blood that has been shed already, perhaps because it was shed in hate, with repression, with violence? Given this uncertain future, may the Lord have compassion on us. I don't want to be pessimistic, because I want to tell you that the strength that must sustain us is prayer.

December 31, 1979

[Note: 1980 is the year that Romero was killed and the year that the United Nations considers that there was a state of civil war.]

[293] + THE PROCESS OF LIBERATION

What must be saved above all else is the process of liberation of our people. The people have begun a process that has already cost them a great deal of blood and we can't let it be for nothing. The crisis of this process must be resolved through the success of the process, and this is what we must seek.

January 6, 1980
READINGS: ISAIAH 60:1–6; EPHESIANS 3:2–3A, 5–6;
MATTHEW 2:1–12

[294] + THE MILITARY

You must realize, dear members of the military, that every institution, including the military one, is at the service of the people. It is the good of the people that must order a change in infrastructure and rules in all institutions. Every institution must be willing to undergo changes in accordance with the demands of the good of the people, and not through absurd canons of hierarchy that choke off the aspirations of a whole people.

January 6, 1980

[295] + THOSE WHO GOVERN

I think that those who truly want to govern the people for true good, can count on the sincere participation of the noble people of El Salvador and should not use their name merely as a ladder to move up, and afterward not take the real people into account, the ones that you have to serve from the government.

January 6, 1980

[296] + A CALL TO THE OLIGARCHY

Finally, a call to the oligarchy: I repeat what I said the last time—don't consider me either a judge or an enemy. I am merely the pastor, a brother, a friend to this people who knows of its suffering, of its hunger, of its anguish. In the name of these voices I raise my voice to say: Don't idolize your wealth, don't protect it in such a way that you let everyone else die of hunger. You must share to be happy. Cardinal Lorscheider [of Brazil] told me of a very picturesque comparison, "You have to know to take off your rings so that they don't cut off your fingers." I think this is understandable. Those who don't want to let go of their rings risk having their hands cut off. Those who don't want to give out of love and because of social justice, run the risk of having everything taken away from them violently.

January 6, 1980

[297] + DON'T BECOME FANATICS

All baptized Salvadorans working in politics in such a terrible situation here in El Salvador have to expand their vision of the kingdom of God. They must not become fanatics in small groups, in political parties. Don't become fanatics because you don't look from within this one organization, of this one project, at the whole political panorama of the common good of our people. You have to be a citizen who, from the perspective of Christian hope, understands another who has a different political project, and work together to seek the kingdom of God so that it might be made flesh and be enthroned in El Salvador.

January 13, 1980

READINGS: ISAIAH 2:1–4, 6–7; ACTS 10:34–38; LUKE 3:15–16, 21–22

[298] + DON'T RAISE YOUR VOICE, STRENGTHEN YOUR ARGUMENTS

I want to appeal to the political leaders who speak into the microphones, to not commit the error that I commit: of shouting too much when we have a microphone in front of us. As if these inventions help us not to strain our throats so much! Because when we hear people with microphones in front of them shouting like demagogues, we say, "And what good does the microphone do this man?" I wish that we could have the serenity with which Christ must have spoken, "He will not shout, nor clamor, nor cry out in the streets" [Isaiah 42:2]. There is a saying: "Don't raise your voice, strengthen your arguments." Many times we shout when we don't have good arguments.

January 13, 1980

[299] + THE TRUE LEADER OF LIBERATION

He is the true leader of liberation. Today's first reading presents it in this way, "I have formed you and I have made you the covenant with my people so that you might open the eyes of the blind, free the captives from prison and those that live in darkness from the underground prisons." It is a language that we can understand and that can be translated into modern terms: the oppressed! Christ came for the oppressed of all classes. And all who want to liberate the people from oppression will not find any other leader greater than Christ, the only liberator.

January 13, 1980

[300] + LIVE REALITY IN COMMUNION

The Christian Base Communities and the bishop have to live reality in communion, because we are not competent as a base community to decide on concrete options. In the current reality, there are, I think, three options presented to us: that of the government, that of the oligarchy, and that of the popular organizations. Everyone is free to choose the option that they prefer. But, as Church, we do have to point out, in any of the options, the criterion from the Gospel of directing it toward the good of the people. No option should be chosen which looks for personal benefits or for that of the group and, much less, one which attempts to maintain selfishness that attacks the people. Rather from this tribune of the Christian community, the pastor and the Christian communities have the obligation to not take sides, but to be Christian consciousness among our people, precisely to orient everything so that this people become a reflection of the kingdom of God here on earth.

January 13, 1980

[301] + THOSE WHO MAINTAIN THE UNJUST SOCIAL STRUCTURES

We have to condemn the structure of sin in which we live, this overwhelming power that pressures, sadly, many people into taking radical and violent options. Those responsible are, precisely, those who maintain these unjust social structures, who make people lose hope that this could be done another way besides through violence. They have to think about whether, if we want to avoid people moving underground, toward violence, toward so much disorder, they have to begin by eliminating the great disorder of their selfishness and their social injustice.

January 13, 1980

[302] + THERE IS STILL TIME TO TAKE OFF YOUR RINGS

The oligarchy is trying to organize and expend its forces to defend its interests. Again, in the name of our people and of our church, I make a new call for you to listen to the voice of God and share gladly with everyone your power and wealth, instead of provoking a civil war that will drown us in blood. There is still time to take off your rings so that they don't take your whole hand.

January 13, 1980

[303] + IT OUGHT TO BE AT THE SERVICE OF THE PEOPLE

The government Junta ought to find an effective way to order an immediate end to so much indiscriminate repression, because the Junta is also responsible for the blood, the pain of so many people. The military, especially the security forces, ought to put aside the rage and hate they show when they persecute people. They ought to demonstrate with actions that they are in favor of the majority and that the process that they have begun is of a popular nature. All of you, or many of you, have your origins in the people, because of which the institution of the army ought to be at the service of the people. Don't destroy the people; don't be the ones to cause the greater and more painful outbreaks of violence with which a repressed people could justly respond.

January 20, 1980

READINGS: ISAIAH 62:1–5; 1 CORINTHIANS 12:4–11; JOHN 2:1–12

[304] + THE GUERRILLA

To these popular organizations, and especially, those of a military and guerrilla nature, whatever their tendency, I also say: Stop these acts of violence and terrorism, which many times are meaningless, and that themselves provoke even more violent situations.

January 20, 1980

[305] + LET'S AVOID CIVIL WAR

Dear brothers and sisters, I want to issue a call to all the sectors of the country so that we might head off a civil war and, in doing so, achieve authentic justice in our country. To do that, it is essential for all of us to be willing to share with the rest what we are and what we have, and to participate, as we are able, in creating an economic-political structure that, in accord with the plan of God, favors all Salvadorans equally.

January 20, 1980

[306] + A CALL TO THOSE WHO DO NOT PARTICIPATE

I issue a call to the sector that is not organized, that up until now has stayed on the outside of political events but is suffering their consequences, so that, as Medellín recommends, it act in favor of justice as far as it is able and not continue to be passive due to fear of the sacrifices and personal risks implicit in any bold and truly effective action. If it does not, then it will also be responsible for the injustice and the dire consequences it will bring.

January 20, 1980

[307] + AS PASTOR AND AS A CITIZEN...

As pastor and as a Salvadoran citizen, I feel deep pain that they continue to massacre the organized sector of our people only because of the fact that they go out into the streets in an orderly fashion to ask for justice and liberty.

January 27, 1980
READINGS: NEHEMIAH 8:2–4A, 5–6, 8–10; CORINTHIANS 12:12–30;
LUKE 1:1–4, 4:14–21

[308] + SO MUCH BLOOD THAT HAS BEEN SHED WILL NOT BE IN VAIN

I am sure that so much blood that has been shed and so much pain that has been caused the families of so many victims will not be in vain. This is blood and pain that will water and fertilize new and ever-more numerous seeds for Salvadorans who will become conscious of the responsibility they have to build a more just and humane society and one that will bear fruit in achieving the bold, structural, urgent, and radical reforms that our country needs.

January 27, 1980

[309] + THE CRY OF LIBERATION

The cry of liberation of our people is a clamor that rises up to God and that no one or nothing will be able to stop now.

January 27, 1980

[310] + THOSE WHO FALL IN THE STRUGGLE

We ought to consider that those who fall in the struggle, as long as it is through sincere love for the people and seeking a true liberation, are always among us.

January 27, 1980

[311] + SOLUTIONS THROUGH DIALOGUE

Faced with the horrifying quantity of blood and violence left us by this week's events, I want to make, in the name of the Gospel, a new call to all sectors of Salvadoran society: to leave behind ways of violence and to look more seriously for solutions through dialogue. Such solutions are always possible as long as human-kind does not reject its own rationality and its good will.

January 27, 1980

[312] + THE VIOLENCE OF THE RIGHT

It has been proved once again that violence doesn't build anything, especially the violence of a recalcitrant right that uses as an instrument the repressive violence of the military for violating, in their favor, the sacred human rights of expression and organization that the people already know how to defend. As to the violence of the military, I ought to remind them of their duty to be at the service of the poor and not merely for the privilege of a few. We wonder why they don't repress with equal fury the subversion of the right—which could be better controlled by the security forces. Regarding this intransigent violence of the right, I repeat again the severe admonition of the Church when it is accused of being responsible for the rage and desperation of the people: they are the true cause and creating a real danger of the communism that they hypocritically denounce.

January 27, 1980

[313] + THE POPULAR ORGANIZATIONS

This same Church, which defends that right to organize and supports all that is just in their demands, can't be in agreement with violence so out of proportion to the strength of the organization and with its strategies of destruction and cruelty that make it as repressive as its opposing forces nor with its ideology when it attacks the faith and feelings of our people. On the contrary, it expects from you, the ones who are organized, that you be rational political forces for the common good of the people. A revolution is not killing people, because only God is master of life. A revolution is not painting graffiti on the walls or shouting wildly in the streets. A revolution is reflecting on political projects that better work to create a people that are just and fraternal.

January 27, 1980

[314] + AUDIENCE WITH GOD

This is an invitation to all brothers and sisters; no one is excluded. We all have this intimate sanctuary of conscience where God is waiting for the hour in which you come down to talk to him and decide, in the light of his gaze, your own destiny. How beautiful it is to think that I can have an audience with him whenever I want! That at any moment when I want to retire in prayer, God is waiting for me and listening.

February 10, 1980

READINGS: ISAIAH 6:1–2A, 3–8; 1 CORINTHIANS 15:1–11;

LUKE 5:1–11

[315] + ENCOUNTER WITH GOD

Human beings can't know themselves until they have encountered God. Because of this, we have so many who idolize their own egos, so many who are proud, so many human beings clinging to the self, worshipping false gods. They have not encountered the true God and, because of this, they haven't known his true greatness. And how unfortunate is life when instead of finding the true God, one is adoring a false god: the god of money, the god of pride, the god of pleasure. All of these are false gods!

February 10, 1980

[316] + THE YSAX COMMENTARY

I want to remind you about the commentary on YSAX. Many of you saw on television what it was referring to: We want to mention the appearance of Mr. D'Aubisson because of its falsity, the lies, and deformations. We hope that the military has been able to recognize the falseness of this gentleman who wants to make a torturer a national hero, a person that doesn't concern himself with the disappeared nor the murdered, nor torture, who confuses the text of the statutes of ORDEN with the inverted practice of terrorizing and of killing, and who brings false witnesses that wouldn't deceive even the most ignorant—like the one who said that he was Nicaraguan but confused the Caribbean with the Gulf of Fonseca, or another one who could barely talk. It is obvious that a political project that needs to rely on people of this caliber cannot be good for the people.

February 10, 1980

[*Note:* YSAX is the archdiocesan radio station: Roberto D'Aubisson was founder of the ARENA party and is generally considered to have founded the death squads and named in the U.N. Commission report as ordering the death of Archbishop Romero; ORDEN was the right-wing peasant organization and death squad.]

[317] + POPULAR ORGANIZATIONS

Dear brothers and sisters, I want to take this opportunity to tell you, especially the dear brothers and sisters of the popular political organizations: The demands of the people are very just and we have to keep defending social justice and love of the poor. But, because of this, if we truly love the people and try to defend them, we will not try to take away from them what is most valuable: their faith in God, their love for Jesus Christ, their Christian feelings.

February 10, 1980

[318] + POVERTY IS AN ACCUSATION

Coming down, he spoke to them and that's how the Gospel begins, "Blessed are the poor for yours is the Kingdom of God" [Luke 6:20]. And, in contraposition to these four beatitudes, he denounces why there are poor, why there are people who are hungry, why there are people who suffer. These, who are blessed because they suffer, because they cry, because they are hungry, why do they exist? Today's Gospel is terrible when it points out the causes of these problems, "Woe to you the rich, because you already have your consolation! Woe to you who are satiated because you will be hungry! Woe to you who laugh now, because you will grieve and you will cry!" [Luke 6:24–25]. In the voice of Christ, we hear the echo of all the prophets of the Old Testament. How terrible are the prophets when they denounce those who acquire house after house and property after property and make themselves the owners of the country! The existence, then, of poverty as a lack of what is necessary, is an accusation.

Brothers and sisters, those who say that the bishop, the Church, the priests, have caused the unease in the country, want to cover up reality. Those who have created the great evil are those who have made possible such horrible social injustice in which our people live.

February 17, 1980

READINGS: JEREMIAH 17:5–8; 1 CORINTHIANS 15:12, 16–20; LUKE 6:17, 20–26

[319] + THE POOR AND THE CHURCH

The poor have marked the true path of the Church. A church that doesn't join with the poor to denounce, from the poor, these injustices they are subject to, is not the true Church of Jesus Christ.

February 17, 1980

[320] + A CHURCH ARM-IN-ARM WITH THE POOR

We want a Church that is truly arm-in-arm with the poor people of El Salvador so that we note that every time we move closer to the poor, we discover the true face of the suffering Servant of Yahweh. This is how we come to understand more clearly the mystery of Christ that becomes human and becomes poor for us.

February 17, 1980

[321] + ANNOUNCING THE GOOD NEWS

What else does the Church do? Announce the Good News to the poor. But not in a demagogic sense, as if excluding the rest, rather on the contrary. Those who have heard bad news in secular circles and have lived worse realities, are hearing through the Church the word of Jesus: The kingdom of God is approaching! It is ours. Blessed are you, the poor, because the kingdom of God is yours! And this means there is also Good News to announce to the wealthy: Let them become poor to share with the poor the good things of the kingdom of God that belong to the poor.

February 17, 1980

[322] + THE DENUNCIATION OF THE PROPHETS

The poor majorities of our country find in the church the voice of the prophets of Israel. There exist among us those who sell the just for money and the poor for a pair of sandals—as the prophets said—those that build up violence and spoils in their palaces, those who oppress the poor, those who create conditions for a reign of violence, lying in their marble beds, those who acquire house after house and annex field after field so that they occupy the entire space, are left alone in the country. These texts of the prophets are not distant voices that we read reverently in our liturgies; they are daily realities whose cruelty and intensity we live daily.

February 17, 1980

[323] + THE CHURCH SUFFERS THE SAME FATE AS THE POOR

And because of this, the Church suffers the same fate as the poor: persecution. Our Church glories in having mixed its blood—that of priests, of catechists, and of communities—with the massacres of the people and has always borne the mark of persecution. It is precisely because of this that it is bothersome, that they make up lies about it and that they don't want to hear in it the voice that is crying out against injustice.

February 17, 1980

[324] + SIN

Sin is what killed the Son of God and sin continues to be what brings death to the sons of God. We see this fundamental truth of faith daily in situations in our country. You can't offend God without offending your brothers and sisters. It is not, then, out of pure routine that we repeat once again that there is a structure of sin in our own country. It is sin because it produces the fruits of sin: the deaths of Salvadorans, the quick death through repression or the slow death of structural oppression. Because of this, we have denounced the sin of injustice.

February 17, 1980

[325] + THE ONE WHO DENOUNCES MUST BE WILLING TO BE DENOUNCED

The one who denounces must be willing to be denounced. And if the Church denounces injustices, it is also willing to hear itself being denounced and is obliged to be converted. The poor are the constant cry that denounces, not only social injustice, but also the lack of generosity of our own Church.

February 17, 1980

[326] + POVERTY IS A SPIRITUALITY

Poverty is a spirituality; it is a Christian attitude. It is the willingness of a soul open to God. Because of this, Puebla said that the poor are a hope in Latin America, because they are the most willing to receive gifts from God. Because of this, Christ says with so much emotion: Blessed are the poor, because yours is the kingdom of God! You are the most able to understand what those who are on their knees to false idols and trust in them do not understand. You, who do not have these idols, you who are unable to trust because you don't have love or power, you who are handicapped in all ways—the poorer you are, the more you are the owners of the kingdom of God, as long as you truly live this spirituality. Because the poverty that Jesus Christ dignifies here is not simple material poverty, not having anything—that is bad. It is a poverty that becomes conscious; it is a poverty that accepts the cross and the sacrifice, but not out of conformity, because it knows that it is not the will of God. It also knows that in the measure in which it makes of its poverty a consciousness, a spirituality, a giving, an openness to being used by the Lord, it is becoming holy. From its holiness, it will know how to be the best liberator of its own people. The Church is forging these liberators of the people. You, Christians, in the measure in which your poverty becomes spirituality, in this measure, you all are liberators of our people.

February 17, 1980

[327] + BLESSED ARE THE POOR IN SP

Blessed are the poor in spirit. And many have twisted th
to the point of saying that everyone is poor, even those
oppressing others. This isn't true. In the context of the Gospel
"poor in spirit"—Luke says simply "poor" [Luke 6:20]—is the one
who is lacking, the one who is suffering oppression, the one who
needs God in order to get out of this situation.

February 17, 1980

[328] + THE POLITICAL DIMENSION OF OUR FAITH

Mary also said a few words that today we consider revolutionary:
Throw the powerful off their thrones when they disturb the tranquility of the people. This is the political dimension of our faith.
Mary lived it; Jesus lived it. He was truly a patriot of a people who
were under foreign domination and that he, doubtless, dreamed
of as being free. But, meanwhile, this people had to pay tribute to
Caesar! Give unto Caesar what is Caesar's but don't give Caesar
what belongs to God. Give to God what belongs to God.

February 17, 1980

[329] + THE PRESTIGE OF THE CHURCH

It is not prestige for the Church to get along well with the
powerful. The prestige of the Church is to sense that the poor
feel it to be theirs, feel that the Church lives a dimension on
earth calling everyone—the wealthy, too—to be converted and
save themselves from the world of the poor, because only they
are the blessed ones.

February 17, 1980

[330] + POVERTY IS A COMMITMENT

This is the commitment of being a Christian: following Christ in his incarnation. And if Christ is God in his majesty who becomes a humble man even to dying like a slave on the cross and who lives with the poor, that's what our Christian faith should be like. A Christian who doesn't want to live this commitment of solidarity with the poor is not worthy of being called a Christian.

February 17, 1980

[331] + SHARING THE SAME FATE AS THE POOR

Christ invited us to not be afraid of persecution, because, believe it, brothers and sisters, the ones who commit themselves to the poor have to share the same fate as the poor. And in El Salvador, we already know what the fate of the poor means: to disappear, to be tortured, to be captured, to be found dead.

February 17, 1980

[332] + WHILE THE COWARDS FLEE

I want to congratulate with immense joy and gratitude the priests, who, precisely when they are more committed to the poor, are most defamed. It is precisely when they are most committed to the misery of our people, that more lies are told about them. I want to be joyful with the men and women religious committed to this people, even to the heroism of suffering with them, with the Christian communities, with the catechists, who, while the cowards flee, remain at their posts.

February 17, 1980

[333] + BEATITUDE

Blessed are those who work for political liberation of the earth taking into account the redemption of the one who saves from sin and saves from death.

February 17, 1980

[334] + THE CHURCH OF THE POOR

In the desire of having a Church like this, like the one Christ has presented to us today: a Church of the poor—not because of social class, but rather because it saves through the poor all those who want to be saved. We try to do this in this way, brothers and sisters, in our archdiocese.

February 17, 1980

[335] + WHAT MATTERS ARE THE POOR PEOPLE

What marks for our Church the limits of this political dimension of faith, is precisely the world of the poor. In the different political moments what matters are the poor people. I don't want to go into detail about all the fluctuations of politics in my country; I have preferred to explain to you the deep roots of the Church's behavior in the explosive world of Salvadoran sociopolitics and I have tried to clarify for you the last criterion, which is theological and historical, for the action of the Church in this area: the world of the poor. According to how things are going for the poor people, the Church will be supporting them from its specific nature as Church, supporting one political project or another. The homily is looking in this moment at the nature of the Church; supporting what benefits the poor, as it also denounces everything that is bad for the poor.

February 17, 1980

[336] + LETTER TO THE PRESIDENT OF THE UNITED STATES

Moved by this concern, I have dared to write a letter to President Carter himself and I am going to send it once you give me your opinion.

Mr. President: I am very worried about the news that the government of the United States is studying how to influence the arms race in El Salvador by sending military teams and advisors to train three Salvadoran battalions in logistics, communications, and intelligence. If this information as reported is correct, your contribution and that of your government, rather than favoring greater justice and peace in El Salvador, without a doubt, will worsen the injustice and repression against the people who are organized, who many times have been struggling so that their most fundamental human rights be respected.... As a Salvadoran and archbishop of the diocese of San Salvador, I have the obligation to be sure that faith and justice reign in my country. I ask you—if you truly want to defend human rights—to deny this military aid to the Salvadoran government. Guarantee that your government will not intervene directly or indirectly through pressure—military, economic, diplomatic, etc.—to determine the fate of the Salvadoran people. At this moment, we are living a grave economic/political crisis in our country, but, without a doubt, more and more, the people who have become conscious and organized and, through this, have begun to train themselves to be actors and be responsible for the future of El Salvador are the only ones capable of overcoming the crisis. It would be unjust and deplorable if, because of the intervention of foreign powers, the Salvadoran people become frustrated, are repressed and kept from deciding autonomously about the economic and political path that our country should follow.

February 17, 1980

[337] + A CALL TO THE OLIGARCHY

The most logical thing is for the powerful of the oligarchy to reflect with human and Christian serenity, if this is possible, on the call that Christ makes to them today in the Gospel: Woe to you because tomorrow you will cry! It is better, using again an image you have heard before, to take off your rings before they cut off your hand. Be logical with your human and Christian convictions, and give the people a chance to organize with a sense of justice. Don't try to defend the indefensible.

February 17, 1980

[338] + LET US ORGANIZE THE CONVERSION OF HEARTS

Let us not look for immediate solutions. We can't try to organize everything all at once in a society that has been so badly organized for so long. But, yes, let's organize a conversion of hearts. Some know how to live in the austerity of the desert, they know how to savor the strong redemption of the cross. They know that there is no greater joy than earning your bread with the sweat of your brow and that there isn't a more diabolical sin than to take bread from the hungry.

February 24, 1980

READINGS: DEUTERONOMY 26:4–10; ROMANS 10:8–13; LUKE 4:1–13

[339] + WOE TO THE POWERFUL!

Woe to the powerful when they don't take into account the power of God, the only powerful one, when it has to do with torturing, with killing, with massacring people so that they are subjugated to those in power! What terrible idolatry they are offering the god of power, the god of money! So many lives, so much blood that God, the true God, the author of the life of humankind, will make these idolaters of power pay dearly.

February 24, 1980

[340] + THE GOD OF ALL PEOPLES

And the God of all peoples, also the God of El Salvador, has to be a God like this, one who will also illuminate politics. He is the one who gives us our fields; he is the one who wants the agrarian reform. He is the one who wants a more just division of the goods that El Salvador produces. It is not right that some accumulate riches in their coffers and that the people are left without these gifts of God that he has given for the people.

February 24, 1980

[341] + ENTRY HALL TO THE KINGDOM OF GOD

Let us have faith, let us truly believe and from our faith, let us illuminate our politics, working on our history, let us be mechanisms of fate for our people but let us not create a purely human project, and, even less, one inspired by the devil. It should be a project inspired by God that leads me to believe in Christ and makes me feel that the history of my country is a history of salvation, because Christ is deeply rooted in my family, in all that is my country. May Christ be the light that illuminates everything. This is how the country can become the entry hall to the kingdom of God.

February 24, 1980

[342] + THE OLIGARCHY

The fact that they dynamited the radio station YSAX is symbolic. What does it mean? The oligarchy, upon seeing that there is a danger that it might lose its total control over investments, of agro-exportation and its virtual monopoly of the land, is defending its selfish interests, not with reason, not with popular support, rather using the only thing that it has: money. Money permits it to buy arms and pay mercenaries that are massacring the people and choking off all legitimate expression that clamors for justice.

February 24, 1980

[343] + NO ONE CAN ANY LONGER KILL THE VOICE OF JUSTICE

Social justice is not so much a law that orders distribution. Seen from a Christian perspective, it is an internal attitude like that of Christ, who being wealthy, became poor to share his love with the poor. I hope that this call of the Church doesn't further harden the hearts of the oligarchs, rather that it moves them to conversion. Share what you are and what you have. Don't continue to silence through violence those who are extending this invitation to you; much less, continue killing those of us who are trying to see to it that there is a more just distribution of power and of the wealth of our country. And I say this in first person because this week I got a warning that I am on the list of those to be eliminated next week. But, it is clear that it is no longer possible to kill the voice of justice.

February 24, 1980

[344] + CALL TO THE POPULAR ORGANIZATIONS

My Lenten call for the conversion of the diverse sectors of El Salvador wouldn't be complete if I didn't also say a fond word as a pastor to the popular forces. It is urgent that the popular organizations continue to mature so that they carry out their mission of interpreting the will of the people. The great dignity of our people merits that their suffering and oppression not be twisted, rather that it be channeled to true spirituality of poverty, as we said last Sunday. Poverty is an indictment of the injustices of the country but it also is a spirituality that the poor have in their hands, a great instrument to be holy and pleasing to God. And it means, also, poverty as a commitment, no less than that of Christ who being wealthy committed himself to live with the poor to save them, precisely because of their poverty.

February 24, 1980

[345] + MAY CHRIST BE IN THE MIDST OF OUR POPULAR PROCESS

Let us assure you, brothers and sisters, that Christ is in the midst of our popular process. Let us be sure that Christ not be distant from our history. This is what matters most at this moment in our country: that Christ be the glory of God, the power of God, and that the scandal of the cross and the pain don't make us flee from Christ, avoiding suffering, rather than embracing it.

March 2, 1980

READINGS: GENESIS 15:5–12, 17–18; PHILIPPIANS 3:17 – 4:1;
LUKE 9:28–36

[346] + SIN IS DEATH

This is the way sin is: It is death. Because of this, wherever there is death, there is sin. Death is the clear signal that sin reigns. It is scary that there are so many deaths in our country and that the sacred paths of our earth are ever more saturated with human blood. Sin reigns in El Salvador and the liberators of El Salvador have to begin there: how to root out sin from our ground.

March 2, 1980

[347] + WITHOUT GOD THERE CAN BE NO LIBERATION

To want to maintain social injustice is to want to keep sin enthroned and throw God out. Without God there can be no liberation, and where there is sin, God can't be present. Projects that are created only to maintain scandalous privileges can't be from God.

March 2, 1980

[348] + THEY ARE MORE PRESENT THAN BEFORE

Let's not think, brothers and sisters, that our dead have gone away from us. Their heaven, their eternal reward, perfects them in love. They continue to love the same causes for which they died. This means that, in El Salvador, this liberating force not only counts on those who are still alive, but also it counts on all those they have tried to kill but who are more present than ever in this process of the people.

March 2, 1980

[349] + UNITY WITH GOD

Yesterday when a reporter asked me where I found my inspiration for my work and my preaching, I told him, "It is a timely question because right now I am coming from my spiritual exercises." If it weren't for this prayer and this reflection with which I try to keep myself in unity with God, I wouldn't be any more than what St. Paul calls "a clanging cymbal."

March 2, 1980

[350] + THE ROCK SHOWER OF TRUTH

The truth may be very weak physically like David; but, however big, however well-armed, lies may be, they are no more than a fantastic Goliath that will fall beneath the rock shower of the truth.

March 2, 1980

[351] + THE CHRISTIAN–MARXIST DIALOGUE

It is also interesting the news that in Rome, next October, there will be a dialogue between Christian and Marxist philosophers. This is for those who are so easily scared by Marxism—not from Christian motives but from selfish interests, because we have never seen so much anticommunist zealousness as when they see their selfish interests in danger. But, yes, there can be a dialogue, not to cede in the principles of faith, but rather to understand what is meant today by communism, by Marxism. And, many times, those who are most scared of the great evils of communism refuse to see the great evils of capitalism that are martyring our people.

March 2, 1980

[352] + THIS IS A PEOPLE THAT MAKES YOU RESPECT IT

The popular organizations are being destroyed; we already know by what tendencies. Because a disorganized people is a mass that can be toyed with; but a people that organizes itself and defends its values, its justice, is a people that makes you respect it.

March 2, 1980

[353] + THE CRY OF LIBERATION

The earth has a great deal of God in it, and, because of this, it groans when the unjust monopolize it and don't leave land for the others. The agrarian reforms are a theological necessity. A country's land can't be concentrated in a few hands; it has to be given to everyone so all participate in the blessings of God on this earth. Each country has its promised land in the territory that geography gives it. But we always ought to see—and not ever forget—the theological reality that land is a sign of justice, of reconciliation. There cannot be true reconciliation of our people with God as long as there is not a just distribution, as long as the goods of the land of El Salvador don't benefit all Salvadorans and make them happy.

March 16, 1980

READINGS: JOSHUA 5:91A, 10–12; 2 CORINTHIANS 5:17–21; LUKE 15:1–3, 11–32

[354] + PRIDE

There is nothing so opposed to reconciliation as pride. There are those who think that they are clean and pure, who think that they have the right to point to others as the cause of all the injustice and are not capable of looking inside and seeing that they also had a part in the country's disorder.

March 16, 1980

[355] + THE CHRIST LEFT BY THE SIDE OF THE ROAD

How much terror has been sown in our people that even friends betray their friends when they see them in trouble! If we only realized that the person in need is Christ, the one who has been tortured, the one who has been imprisoned, the one who has been murdered; and if, in the body of each person thrown in so undignified a fashion by the side of the road, we were to see the Christ who was left there, I would wager a golden medal that we would pick him up tenderly and we would kiss him and we would not be ashamed of him.

March 16, 1980

[356] + THE MILLIONS AREN'T WORTH ANYTHING

There is much we need to bring to the consciousness of human beings today, especially in those that torture and kill and prefer their wealth to human beings, so that they realize that their millions from the land are no good, that they aren't worth more than human beings. Humankind is Christ and in humankind, seen with faith and treated with faith, we see Christ the Lord.

March 16, 1980

[357] + THEY TOUCH THE VERY HEART OF GOD

Once more the Lord asks Cain: Where is your brother Abel? And although Cain answers the Lord that he is not his brother's keeper, the Lord replies, "The blood of your brother is crying out to me from the earth. Because of that, this land curses you; it has opened its mouth to receive from your hands the blood of your brother. Although you till the land, it will not reward you with its fruitfulness; you will wander lost in the world," words from Genesis chapter 4 [10–12]. And this continues to be the principal concern of the Church, this is what obliges it to raise its voice incessantly, untiringly, week after week, as if crying in the wilderness. There is nothing so important to the Church as human life, as the human being. Especially, the person of the poor and oppressed, who besides being human beings, are divine beings, so that, as Jesus said, anything that is done for them, he regards as done for him. And this blood, the blood, the death which is there beyond all politics, touches the very heart of God and makes it impossible for either the agrarian reform, or the nationalization of the bank, or other measures that have been promised to bear fruit if there is blood.

March 16, 1980

[358] + NOTHING MATTERS SO MUCH TO ME AS HUMAN LIFE

This is the fundamental message of my preaching: Nothing matters so much to me as human life. It is something so serious and so profound, more than the violation of any other human right, because it is the life of the sons of God, and because this blood only negates love, awakens new hate and makes peace and reconciliation impossible. What is most needed here today is an end to the repression.

March 16, 1980

[359] + NOTHING VIOLENT CAN BE LASTING

Someone criticized me implying that I wanted to bring together in one group the popular forces and the guerrilla forces. My mind has always been very clear as to the differences. To them, then, and to others who promote violent solutions, I want to issue a call for understanding. Know that nothing violent can be lasting. Know also that rational solutions are still within the realm of human possibilities, and that, above everything else, is the word of God. Today it shouts at us: reconciliation!

March 16, 1980

[360] + WHILE I AM GATHERING THE CRIES OF THE PEOPLE

I already know that there are many who are scandalized by these words and want to accuse the Church of having abandoned the preaching of the Gospel to get involved in politics. But I don't accept this accusation, rather I make an effort so that everything that the Second Vatican Council, the meetings of Puebla and Medellín, have wanted to promote doesn't stay in the texts to be studied in a theoretical sense but rather that we live them and translate them in this conflictive reality so that we preach the gospel as we should for our people. Because of this, I ask the Lord all week, while I am gathering the clamor of the people and the pain of so much crime, the ignominy of so much violence, that I be given the right words to console, to denounce, to call to repentance; and, although it continues to be a voice crying out in the wilderness, I know that the Church is making the effort to carry out its mission.

March 23, 1980

READINGS: ISAIAH 43:16–21; PHILIPPIANS 3:8–14; JOHN 8:1–11

[361] + TRANSCENDENCE

What is transcendence? I think that I may repeat this idea too much, but I never tire of doing so. Because we often run the risk of wanting to get out of immediate situations and we forget that the immediate solution can be a patch but not a true solution. The true solutions have to fit into the definitive project of God. All the solutions that we might want to suggest for a better land distribution, for a better administration in El Salvador, for a political organization conformed to the common good of the Salvadorans, will always have to be sought in the achievement of definitive liberation.

March 23, 1980

[362] + THE ARCHBISHOP'S LINE

I don't like it when they say the Archbishop's line—I don't have a personal line. I am trying to follow the line of the great achievements of the Church—and I am glad that the Pastoral Commission studies this as a diocesan project—that I already received as a precious inheritance from Bishop Chavez and that we are trying to put into practice with great success in the communities that take it seriously.

March 23, 1980

[363] + HYMN TO THE DIVINE SAVIOR [SALVADOR] OF THE WORLD

And, on a sympathetic note, also from our diocesan life, is that a composer and poet has written a beautiful hymn for our Divine Savior. Soon we will be introducing it, "The explosive songs of joy vibrate/ I am going to meet my people at the cathedral/ Thousands of voices join together today / to sing at the fiesta of our patron saint." And then there follow verses that the people feel very strongly. The last one is very beautiful, "But the gods of power and wealth, oppose transfiguration / Because of this, now, you, Lord, are the first / to raise your arm against oppression."

March 23, 1980

[Note: This hymn was written by Guillermo Cuéllar and is part of the Salvadoran Folk Mass.]

[364] + STOP THE REPRESSION!

I want to make a special plea to the men of the army, and, specifically, to the rank-and-file of the National Guard, of the police, to
those in the barracks. Brothers, we are part of the same people.
You are killing your own brother and sister peasants and when
you are faced with an order to kill given by a man, the law of God
must prevail; the law that says: Thou shalt not kill. No soldier is
obliged to obey an order against the Law of God. No one has
to obey an immoral law. And it is time that you recover your
consciences and obey your consciences over an order that is
sinful. The Church, defender of human rights, of the law of God,
of human dignity, of the human being, cannot remain silent in
the face of such abomination. We want the government to take
seriously the idea that the reforms are meaningless when they are
stained with so much blood. In the name of God, then, and in the
name of this suffering people whose laments rise up to heaven
each day more tumultuously, I plead with you, I pray you, I order
you, in the name of God: Stop the repression!

March 23, 1980

[365] + THE LAST WORDS

That this immolated Body and this Blood sacrificed for human-kind, may nourish our bodies and our blood in suffering and in pain, like Christ, not for its own sake, but rather to give the concepts of justice and peace to our people. Let us join together then, intimately in faith and hope in this moment of prayer for Doña Sarita and for ourselves...[at this moment the shot rang out].

March 24, 1980

[*Note*: The Mass Romero was celebrating that day, Monday, March 24, 1980, at the Divina Providencia Chapel was for the one-year anniversary of the death of newspaper editor Jorge Pinto's mother.]